AY

10-19-71

Change Your Handwriting, Change Your Life

Change Your Handwriting, Change Your Life

CHARLOTTE P. LEIBEL

STEIN AND DAY/*Publishers*/New York

First published in 1972
Copyright © Charlotte P. Leibel 1972
Library of Congress Catalog Card No. 72-163354
All rights reserved
Published in Canada by Saunders of Canada Ltd.
Designed by Bernard Schleifer
Printed in the United States of America
Stein and Day/*Publishers*/7 East 48 Street, New York, N.Y. 10017
ISBN 0-8128-1416-9

Contents

II. SELF-CORRECTION THROUGH HANDWRITING

*Each man is his own absolute lawgiver,
the dispenser of glory or gloom to himself, the
decreer of his life, his reward, his punishment.*
—One of the three truths of Theosophy

Introduction

Reading a book cannot make you a handwriting analyst any more than reading any book can make you an authority. But it can start you thinking in a new vein. It can make you aware of some of the things you did not know.

This book on handwriting analysis has no intention of making you an expert in this field. It merely serves to point out some of the characters in your handwriting that display your negative characteristics and which you would like to correct.

It is not my belief alone that strokes which indicate a positive attitude can be acquired through consistent practice. There are many authorities in the field of graphology who are of similar opinion.

You will find this book to have two major sections:
1. The technique of handwriting analysis.
2. How to correct and abandon the negative aspects of your writing and how to develop and acquire a positive approach to living.

Miami Beach, Florida　　　　　　　　　　CHARLOTTE P. LEIBEL

Analyzing
Your
Handwriting

A History of Graphology

From earliest times, the finest minds of mankind have recognized the relation of handwriting to character. While many famous people in history and literature showed a keen interest in the analysis of character through handwriting and made individual estimates without any rules or laws, the first treatise on this subject was written in 1632 by an Italian physician, Camille Baldo. It was called *How to Know the Nature and Qualities of a Person by Looking at a Letter He Has Written.*

However, the real origin of modern graphology is to be found in France. In 1830 a learned churchman, the Abbé Flandrin, enlarged upon the book by Baldo. His work attracted many men of scholarship. A study group was formed and enthusiasm for graphology spread. In 1875, a pupil of Abbé Flandrin, the Abbé Michon, coined the word *graphology*, which means the science of writing; he passed his mastership on to Jamin, with whom modern graphological work began.

In 1896, Ludwig Klages, a physician who founded the Graphological Society, brought this field of study to Germany with scientific and governmental acceptance. He was the first to create a complete and systematic theory of graphology. His system resulted in the present graphological method now recognized and used in Europe as a psychodiagnostic instrument. Apart from Klages, most of the more outstanding modern work was done by Robert Saud of England and Max Pulver of Switzerland. Pulver enlarged and modernized the graphological findings of Klages and developed the connection between graphology and the psychology of the unconscious (psychoanalysis).

In Germany handwriting analysis is used more than any other diagnostic device, such as the Rorschach Inkblot Test and other personality tests, and there are nine universities teaching graphology and two thousand practicing graphologists. In other European countries, especially France and Holland, handwriting analysts are widely employed by business, educational and psychiatric organizations.

However, graphology in the U.S. has been received with skepticism and neglected until recently. It is now slowly and surely being recognized as a useful diagnostic tool and is accepted in academic and scientific circles as an expressive movement which reveals personality. For those who may become further interested in this subject, there are many excellent books on the interpretation of handwriting by Louise Rice, Nadya Olyanova, Klara Roman, Ulrich Sonneman and Irene Marcuse. In England, books have been written by Hans Jacoby.

In addition to determining the personality and character of an individual, it has been found that handwriting also expresses significant indications of the mental and physical health of the writer and thus can be useful to psychologists, psychiatrists and physicians. In 1952, *This Week* magazine in an article entitled "Now Doctors Examine Your Handwriting" had this to say: "After generations of scoffing, medical experts have now become convinced that it is possible to learn important facts about a person from a specimen of his handwriting. Every day fresh confirmation of the value of handwriting . . . is coming from doctors and psychologists." In the March 27, 1969, issue of the *New England Journal of Medicine*, the efficacy of L-Dopa therapy in Parkinson's disease was shown through handwriting samples by comparing the signature of the writer before the onset of the disease, during the disease, and after taking medication.

Since graphology has been found to be of great value in vocational guidance and personnel selection in business, large industrial firms throughout the United States are employing graphologists. The Central Intelligence Agency has long used handwriting analysis in conjunction with other types of tests to discern character and personality traits. Graphology is used in marriage counseling, in child guidance, and in crime detection; it can even help historians to obtain an unbiased picture of a person who is no longer alive. It has helped many thousands of people to attain self-understanding, thereby enabling them to develop their potentialities and overcome their weaknesses.

A recent development in graphology has been the successful use of it therapeutically in France since 1930. Its efficacy was tested clinically at the Sorbonne by two French scientists, Dr. Pierre Janet and Professor Charles Henry. When a writer was made aware of certain features in his handwriting which were caused by neurotic inhibition, he was shown how to change such features in his writing; thereby his inner conflicts were brought out into the open and eventually resolved and mitigated.

Basic Concepts

1. Handwriting is an expressive movement expressing the individuality of the writer, and is consistent with other expressions of personality.

2. Handwriting is unique and never duplicated, for there are no two handwritings alike. Everything and everyone has his own individuality, and man above all living creatures has the most outstanding individuality.

3. Writing is performed to a large extent by unconscious action; we are not conscious of how we write, but are only concerned in conveying a message. In the act of writing we register positive and negative signs automatically and leave a permanent mark, revealed by some odd trait in the writing, of what the subconscious knows. This is the reason why a person cannot cover up the things that lie deep in his character.

4. The term *handwriting* is incorrect, because a person can learn how to write with his toes, or even with his head and mouth,

and will produce the same letter formations normally produced by means of his hands. This proves beyond a reasonable doubt that individual handwriting is not produced by manual skill but is a product of our individuality.

5. Handwriting is really brain or mind writing. You have to give your whole attention to writing. Every nervous and muscular movement originates in the brain. The hand merely holds the pen. It is the brain which directs the movement of the hand and which is responsible for the manner in which you form your letters and space your lines.

6. No single trait or feature of handwriting can be interpreted without reference to all others, even though the graphologist may set them apart, and there is no other projective technique that offers such advantages as a sole means of total personality assessment.

SYMBOLISM

While it is generally known that the letters of the alphabet are symbolic representations of the sounds universally possible to the human voice, it is not so generally known that they are shaped to picture basic ideas subjected constantly to new interpretations. One of the first basic ideas in the history of man was the development of religious concepts which later became a symbol of communication with others.

Handwriting is a sequence of written symbols bearing a message from the writer to the reader—the written counterpart of speech. The graphologist sees this, but he sees much more. He sees written signs as a symbol of inner psychological processes that transmit messages frequently not even understood by the writer. A human body has developed through a process of evolution over many millions of years and so has the human soul. According to the late Dr. Carl J. Jung, images from primitive eras have remained in the depths of the human soul and now appear as archetypes.

Max Pulver, the Swiss graphologist who linked graphology with the discoveries of the psychology of the unconscious, emphasized the strong symbolic element in handwriting, especially illuminating the problem of what space symbolizes in the writer's mind. He said, "The writer is faced by the empty paper which he has to fill. He has to start somewhere on the left, to work up and down and to go to the right. Now, it is inherent in human nature and confirmed by the psychology of the unconscious that every problem of form and space becomes symbolic in the individual's mind of his own position in the different spheres of space and time, that is to say, his spiritual, social and material world.

"And so the point along the line of the writing at which the moving pen of the writer arrives becomes a symbol of his own position in the world around him: to the left of this point lies the past, origin, mother and childhood; to the right lies the work to be done, the future, the writer's fellowmen and the social world.

"Movements upward above the extension of the short letters (*a, e, i, o, m, s, u, v,* etc.) symbolize gravitation toward spiritual and intellectual spheres; movements below symbolize the dive into the material, subhuman and subconscious world.

"Thus the manuscript becomes a symbol of the writer's attitude to the past and the future, to himself and to others, to the spiritual, social and material world, to airy dreams and to subconscious impulses."

THE WRITING FIELD

SEX AND AGE OF THE WRITER

Before proceeding with an analysis of a handwriting, the sex and age of the writer must be determined. It has been established by many experiments that the sex and age of a person cannot in every case be ascertained through his handwriting for the following reasons:

1. Medical research has shown that every human being has masculine and feminine characteristics in both a psychological and a biological sense. Hence, there are feminine men who write like women and masculine women who write like men.

2. Some people reach considerable maturity while still quite young and will write like adults, while others will be surprisingly immature and even infantile at fifty and will write like children.

Form Level or Quality

Before starting the evaluation of any feature of a script, a thorough examination of the form level must take place. The form level gives us an overall impression of the writing and is to be evaluated on the following three components of the script:

1. Distribution of spaces (general layout).
   Clearness of spaces with harmony and balance in the proportion of the script itself. This shows that the writer is clear-minded and has a distinct conception and plan before he starts something.

2. Naturalness or artificiality.
   The act of writing must have been performed as a means of expression and not for the sake of writing, or in order to impress by form. A speedy script is usually natural.

3. Originality of letter forms.
   The letters should reveal maturity but no eccentricity. This

is measured by the degree to which you have overcome conventional school patterns. There must be simplification without impairing legibility.

As a result of these considerations, we determine the quality or form level as being:

a. average or medium
b. above average (superior)
c. below average (inferior)

The higher the form level of the handwriting, the more the evaluation tends to indicate positive character traits, found in the positive columns. The lower the form level, the more it tends to indicate negative traits of character to be found in the negative columns. In medium or average form level, the character traits will have positive as well as negative indications.

I really believe he can be right on time if he tried

Average form level

NATURALNESS: Good.
SPACING: Good between words, medium between lines.
ORIGINALITY: OF FORMS: Medium, adheres to conventional school pattern.

I would say that
Alice makes some
very good points

Above-average form level

NATURALNESS: Good.

SPACING: Good between words and lines.

ORIGINALITY OF FORMS: Good; see capital *A*, *I*, and small *s*, *g*, *t*, and *d*.

Florence and Mr.
Brown have to

Below-average form level

NATURALNESS: Very unnatural writing, artificial flourishes; writer wants to impress by form.

SPACING: Poor between lines and words.

ORIGINALITY OF FORMS: Letter forms are conventional.

R *hythm*

The definition of rhythm is regular, repeated movement. This implies steadiness of beat with unbroken constancy. Each person has his own individual rhythm and it is unique. When he becomes aware of this uniqueness in him, an individual is better able to direct his life. Since every individual is different, each must follow his individual expression of the rhythm operating in him. To understand this law, it must be explored in terms of individual motivation and setting.

Since handwriting is an expression of a living organism, the presence or absence of rhythm is one of its most essential characteristics. Rhythm in handwriting is an expression not only of your vitality but your entire character, its force and impact, and your capacity for life's experience. When you function naturally and properly, psychologically and physically, your handwriting will show rhythm; that is, your handwriting will be balanced, harmonious and fluent.

If your natural functioning is disturbed, there will be disturbances in the rhythmic distribution and periodicity of the writing elements; that is, your writing will reveal extreme unevenness with changes or fluctuations in the slant, pressure, size, spacing, base line, speed, regularity, etc., giving the impression of restless, excited and unbalanced movements.

While there may be irregularities in the handwriting, if they are shown at equal intervals it is not considered unrhythmic. Monotonous, stereotyped regularity has no rhythm.

RHYTHMIC (EVEN) WRITING

Positive Example	Description	Indication
Are you sure of the facts,	Writing movements showing a calm, even flow, smooth and free from disturbances.	Inner harmony, quiet balance of the mind, able to preserve equanimity and serenity even if subjected to strong and exciting stimuli, able to control impulses. Emotionally stable.
Put all of them on the second	Rhythmic with regular writing.	Strength of will and perseverance.

Negative Example	Description	Indication
one matter of importance is	Rhythmic writing, even flow.	People of composure who are difficult to excite because they are dull, indifferent and apathetic in their reactions.
she wanted a larger picture of	Unrhythmic writing, extremely uneven, with variations in slant, spacing, regularity, etc.	Hastily excitable and upset emotionally, highly impressionable; nervous disturbances, inhibition, discord, loses inner balance. Found in the handwriting of psychoneurotics, psychotics and those physically ill.

Pressure

Pressure is the degree of energy forced by the pen on the writing surface. In determining pressure, we must ascertain the type of pen used, because a person chooses the pen suited to his personality. Those who use a pen with a fine line will produce a light pressure and those who write with a broad nib produce a heavy pressure. Pressure can only be determined when the writing is in ink, preferably dark blue or black. It cannot be accurately determined if the writing is in pencil. To ascertain pressure, use a magnifying glass.

The natural or proper place for the application of pressure is on the downstroke. The varying pressures of the downstroke movements express the core of the personality. Under magnification, a ball-point pen reflects pressure in a different way from a fountain pen, but since the ball-point pen is being increasingly used, we must study the pressure carefully and do the best we can. Pressure symbolizes the libido. The libido means all those mental and physical energies that drive us to activity. Pressure indicates the state of health, vitality, willpower and depth of feeling of the writer. A lack of pressure indicates a lack of energy or libido.

There are many pressures—heavy, medium heavy, light, medium light, weak and light, pasty, uneven and wavering, periodic, smeary and muddy, horizontal and displaced—and the sharpness of strokes must also be considered.

H E A V Y   P R E S S U R E

Positive Example	*Description*	*Indication*
a market for a	Heavy pressure.	Physical strength, vitality, energy, activity, depth of emotion, driving power, strong sex drive, usually successful in anything tried, aggressive, spontaneous.
the large hat	With regularity.	Willpower.
take it with	With quick tempo.	Much energy and ambition.

Negative Example	*Description*	*Indication*
a market for	Heavy.	Aggressiveness, stubbornness, depression, excitement, impulsive, self-assertive, materialistic, pugnacious.
tried and tested	With hooks.	Aggressiveness that is irritating and will interfere with full success.
Robert Smith	With large capitals.	Drive becomes selective, selfish, self-centered; while successful, individual becomes unhappy over the many people stepped upon in climbing to the top.
has this gone up?	Extremely heavy.	Individual living at too high tension with forcefulness and aggressiveness, wasting vitality and energy, which can undermine health. Emphatic, forceful, domineering, sensual.

MEDIUM HEAVY PRESSURE

The majority of people use this pressure.

Positive Example	Description	Indication
would have done	Halfway between heavy and medium light pressure.	Average drive, mildly successful, composed, adaptable, unaffected, conforming.

LIGHT PRESSURE

It is produced by gliding over the surface of the paper with the least possible effort. The libido is minimal.

Positive Example	Description	Indication
By now one of them is ready	With above-average form level.	Refinement, gentle, sensitive, interest in mental and spiritual or inspirational things, rather than desires. Elasticity, adaptability, fine character.
time and tide wait for us	With connected writing, high *t* crossing and *i* dots, good spacing.	Has intuition but does not trust it, must find reasons for everything. Because judgment is good, intuition can be trusted.
on many trips	Combined with shading.	Intuitive.

Negative Example	Description	Indication
The average was	Light pressure.	Lack of sensual urge, sexual desire is weak or absent, no natural driving power, lack of will, little impulse for combating life, lack of energy, fatigue, dislikes exertion, wants to fit in without a struggle or overcoming obstacles, weak constitution, easily influenced by the world around him, often fails.
for he is getting along	With below average form level, poor traits.	An unstable person.
is much as here	Light and weak, almost pressureless.	Weakness of health, lack of vigor, fearful and timid, lack of interest in sexuality; suggestibility, and poor willpower, often seen in the handwriting of invalids and those physically exhausted, anemics, low blood pressure, extremely sensitive, easily discouraged, no desire for anything material, wants to be relieved of responsibilities.
has far to go in	With irregularity.	Weak will, pliability, fearfulness, sensitivity, inferiority.
he followed in a	With extreme rightward slant.	Mild, affectionate nature but relatively weak personality.

HORIZONTAL OR DISPLACED PRESSURE

In this pressure, there is systematic displacement of the normal pressure from the downstroke to the side stroke. This is where pressure does not belong, according to psychophysical energy.

Positive Example	Description	Indication
the meeting is	Emphasis of pressure on side or horizontal strokes.	Sex drive is sublimated and harnessed so that it leaves one free for creative work; often seen in the handwriting of genius.
One after the other	With inferior form level.	Sexual maladjustment; sex energies are perverted or abnormal.
accept this for	With uneven pressure.	Different kinds of disturbance, especially mental abnormalities.

PASTY PRESSURE

This pressure has an equal thickness in up and down strokes; there are no light or dark gradations; strokes are uniform with no shading. It can be heavy or light, according to the force or energy used by the writer. When it is heavy it looks like a dark stream of paste squeezed out of a hole.

Positive Example	Description	Indication
from a lighter	Equal thickness of pressure in up and down strokes, individually shaped.	Impressionable, impressed by rich colors and soft fabrics; those close to nature, warmth. Creative artists.

Negative Example	Description	Indication
Every day	Equal thickness of pressure in up and down strokes.	Motivated by pleasure; lack of spirituality; sensual, crude, anxious.
allow for	With slow writing. no individuality in the script.	Lazy, indolent and sensual; crudeness, lack of spirituality.

you go along   With short lower loops.

Attracted to the opposite sex, enjoys the preparation, i.e., flirting, kissing, but has no interest in the sex act because of some incapacity.

PERIODIC PRESSURE

Periodic pressure is a sudden pressure on an occasional stroke. It has a negative indication.

Negative Example	*Description*	*Indication*
Blanche will go	Pressure on an occasional stroke.	Irritability, emotional imbalance, a violent nature. Sexual excitement in a very passionate type.

SHARPNESS OF THE STROKES

Sharpness of the strokes symbolizes rationality. It is found in fine, thin, pressureless writing with wide or narrow loops, not filled with ink; the strokes have clear-cut edges.

Positive Example	*Description*	*Indication*
the afternoon	Sharp strokes.	Idealism, spirituality, refinement, analytical mind, ability to criticize, people in the clergy, keen mind, sensitive to aesthetic things, art, music; professional critics will show this pressure. Intensity of thought.

Negative Example	*Description*	*Indication*
the afternoon		Coldness, asceticism, hypercritical, intellect, resentment.

Slant

Slant in handwriting is the angle which the downstrokes form with the base line. There are three basic slants—rightward, vertical or upright, leftward or backhand—and they express respectively compliance, self-reliance and defiance.

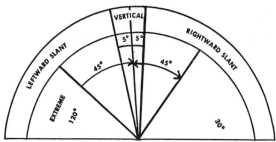

Slant is the indicator of your emotional makeup and your relation to the past, present and future. The three slants in their varying degrees express the different approaches to life, i.e., the different attitudes of your mind toward people, objects or aims, either introverted or extroverted or a combination of both. The degree may be determined by the degree of the slant.

The range of the slant between 30 degrees (extreme right) and 120 degrees (extreme left) indicates the degrees between impulsivity and self-control. A perfectly even slant is rarely found in one specimen of handwriting. When upper and lower extensions have exactly the same angle, the writer either has supercontrol or has lost his natural attitude because of inner or outer pressure. While the slant in a handwriting can be changed if one exerts effort to do so, a change of slant from extreme left to extreme right and vice versa should be avoided.

RIGHTWARD SLANT

As writing proceeds from left to right, the natural tendency is to the right-hand side. Rightward slant symbolizes concern with society and implies a natural personality. The more the slant tends to the right, the less control there is over the emotions and the greater the social instinct.

Positive Example	Description	Indication
almost every	Moderately rightward.	Social, friendly, emotional, affectionate, outgoing, extroverted, warm nature, active, wants to keep moving ahead, needs people, spontaneous, sensitive, ruled by the emotions, interested in the world and action, adaptable, expressive and demonstrative in feeling but does not go to extremes; found in writing of salesmen, teachers and social workers.
to bind them	Rightward with simplified letters.	An objective mind.
the level of	Moderately rightward with rounded and graceful letters.	An enterprising and progressive mind and a sociable nature.
she may be	Moderately rightward with large rhythmic quick writing.	Ambition, steady, enthusiastic, well integrated, sociable.

Negative Example	Description	Indication
one and	Very large letters, rounded, with rightward slant.	Unrestrained impulse, an impatient and unconcentrated nature. Though with strong and passionate feelings, naturally is inconsiderate and thoughtless.
college grades	Extreme rightward slant.	Lack of control and discipline, active, impulsive, impatient, restless, hasty, thoughtless, immoderate, excitable, can be hysterical; distractibility, dependency on outside world, hates to be alone, supersensitive, off balance with people and day-to-day matters, frequently exhausted, rapid likes and dislikes, emotionally expressive and demonstrative, prone to accidents, sharp mood swings from elation to depression, reacts without thinking, romantic, hurls self into the environment and is dissipated by it. Found in handwritings of alcoholics or users of drugs. In the writing of the alcoholic and drug user, the letters will be misshapen and the base line downward.
daily life	Extreme rightward with light pressure.	Relatively weak personality.
only one out	Extreme rightward with small writing.	Very excitable, lacks resistance against impressions.

Thntsmhii Trg	Extreme rightward slant, increasing in tilt with each succeeding word.	Uncontrolled behavior, can lose footing, low frustration tolerance, gives up connection with reality and will falsify actualities to meet the demand, a disposition to drift into alcoholism.
out of the	Right slant with pasty pressure.	Lack of sexual inhibitions.
sinu whu was	Right slant with irregularity and neglected writing.	Hasty person.
many among	Diminishing rightward slant at end of words.	May start impulsively but manages gradually to control the emotions.
Those w	Capital letter more rightward than following letters.	Starts impulsively but soon regains self-control.
There	Capital letter vertical followed by right-slanting letters.	Writer overcomes his initial inhibition.
Patty King	Two slants, rightward and vertical	Versatility, may be informal and spontaneous to close friends but formal and aloof to strangers.

VERTICAL (UPRIGHT) SLANT

This slant symbolizes neutrality, self-reliance and poise, and represents intellectual control. The slant is considered vertical if it varies 5 degrees leftward or rightward.

Positive Example	Description	Indication
get help for	Vertical or upright.	Mind rules the emotions (dominance of reason), highly critical, self-control, self-reliance, self-command, independent, lives in the present, objective, good judgment and reasoning, sustained effort, reserved, poised, well-mannered, has charm.
a grand time was had	With small writing, good form level.	Scholarly mind, high IQ, appreciates order and routine and the aesthetic rather than the sensuous, highly critical, deep thinker, could do scientific work.

Negative Example	Description	Indication
get help for	Vertical or upright.	Past adversity or painful memories caused writer to repress to some degree his affections and spontaneity and there is a need to come to grips with the problem; he has a detached attitude involving tension and anxiety. Self-contained, matter-of-fact, not moved by sentiment nor prone to demonstrate feelings; caution, lacks empathy; egotism, and self-centeredness.
any other way	With heavy pressure.	Holds back a force of emotional energy meant to be outgoing.
was he on the	With unusually tall letters.	Great hunger for prestige, power and position.

most of the time	With compressed letters.	Control of expressiveness accentuated which may affect the health.
they rag	With weak, slow, small, neglected writing, upper and lower zones slight.	A lazy person.

THE LEFT (BACKWARD) SLANT

The left slant symbolizes concern with one's ego. It expresses a loss of naturalness and a lack of spontaneity with some kind of artificiality. The further leftward the slant is away from the vertical, the more the writer is separated and alienated from realities. There is always some kind of barrier between these writers and the outside world. They can have strong family ties and are seldom free from memories of past environmental experiences.

Positive Example	*Description*	*Indication*
what good is it	Left slant, full pasty writing with originality.	Fertile imagination, introspective.
he gave away	Moderate left slant with small size.	Reflective, disciplined, interest in abstractions.

Negative Example	*Description*	*Indication*
far along the	Moderate left slant.	Some inhibition and introversion, ruled by the mind. Self-contained, represses some emotions, reserved, fear of the future.

the first on the

Extreme leftward, backhand.

Introverted, thoughts turn inward, inhibited and repressed, interest is more in things than people, acts aloof; reserved feelings border on an attitude of self-defense following disillusionment or disappointment in financial, sexual, spiritual or social fields; unadaptable. Writer has inner conflicts whose sources lie in early life experience and has built up defenses in the form of defiant or negativistic behavior, opposition to everything. In childhood, writer was probably frustrated and rebuffed.

Only more than feels

Left slant, below-average form level.

Hypocrisy and insincerity.

every one saw her

Left slant, narrow, slow letters and downward base line.

Depressed person who is afraid of facing life and its problems.

maybe it is

Left slant with large writing, thick pointed letters.

Tendency to be cruel.

LEFT-HANDEDNESS

In making a handwriting analysis, there is no difference between right-handed and left-handed writing. Though it would seem that left-handed writers would automatically write backhand, this is not the case. If a left-handed writer writes in the left slant, it is not because he is left-handed but because he has the characteristics indicated in the left slant and no matter which hand he used, he would write leftward. The left-handed writer who writes with a rightward slant has adjusted to the right-handed world. Ambidextrous people can write with either hand, left or right. Because many cases of stuttering have been caused by the parents forcing left-handed children to write with the right hand, this practice should be avoided. It interferes with a natural function.

VARYING OR FLUCTUATING SLANT

The mixed slant indicates a change in the direction of the emotional current. When a writer uses a three-way slant, rightward, leftward and vertical in one specimen of writing (sometimes in one word), he traverses the entire scale of emotional responses and will show the characteristics that go with the varying slants. When the slant varies noticeably, reason is master first and feelings the master next, revealing a battle between the conscious and subconscious mind.

Positive Example	Description	Indication
the disability he	Mixed or varying slant with steady base line and consistent size of letters.	Versatile and adaptable.
spiritual teachings	Mixed or varying slant.	Versatile, impressionable, lively, many interests, likes change and variety. Sometimes, it may reveal a creative genius.

Negative Example	Description	Indication
upon the mind	Varying or mixed slant.	Unstable, unpredictable, indecisive; anxiety, neurosis, emotional changeability, moodiness, inconsistency, depression, frustrated in terms of reaching a goal. The writer is pulled in many directions, uncertain; a lack of willpower prevents him from developing into a consistent character; fickle, dislikes routine and detail, has inner conflicts between love and hate, mind and emotions, impulse and control, the past and the future. Writer is immature and indefinite in reaction, abilities are thwarted, concentration impaired, resulting in nervous fatigue.
knowledge	Varied slants within a word.	Inner conflicts and irresolution.
independently	Varied slant in middle zone; upper and lower zone letters have consistent slant.	Inertia caused by moodiness and lack of will prevents writer from putting his ideas into action; unsteady in progress.
reality	Right slant in upper and lower zones; left slant in middle zone.	Spiritually and instinctively directed toward the outside world but in his personal emotional attitude in everyday life, he is afraid of establishing contacts.
hurry to go there	Varied slants, poor form level, i.e., wavering base line, uneven middle zone and pressure.	Unreliability, instability, moodiness, excessive sensitivity.

Leftward and Rightward Trends

Apart from the slant, writing movements have rightward and leftward tendencies. These tendencies are found in the upper, lower and middle zones, and they can occur in one zone or in all three. Right tendencies and movements are related to a wide writing and left tendencies to a narrow one. If the strokes which normally turn left or right go in the opposite direction, they should be evaluated in the handwriting. Unknowingly everyone stands under the symbolism of the left and right. The left symbolizes the past, the self and introversion. The right symbolizes the future, other people and extroversion. The upright symbolizes the present and independence.

RIGHTWARD TENDENCIES

Rightward tendencies in handwriting signify a free approach to people, events, and actions, spontaneity, the outer life and extroversion.

Positive Example	Description	Indication
P F	In the upper zone.	Experimentation.
d	Letter *d* progressing to the right.	Emancipation, break with the past, protest.
am marble	In the middle zone.	Extroverted inclinations, altruism, urge for human contact, sympathy, sense of enterprise.

fine age you	In the lower zone.	Instinctive understanding of others, dexterity, extroversion.
you	In lower zone with short, sharp strokes.	Initiative, aggressiveness.
y	Omitted loop in lower zone.	Increased concentration.

Negative Example	Description	Indication
P f	In upper zone.	Lack of contemplation, rash judgment, suggestibility.
t	Extended *t* bars.	Desire for power.
am marble	In middle zone.	Restlessness, weakness, wastefulness, spreading oneself thin, easily influenced.
am	With exaggerated finals.	Prodigality.
extend towards	Long finals in narrow writing.	Pretended generosity.
are	Finals straight, with pressure.	Suspicion.
y	In lower zone, with uncertain downstrokes.	Uncertainty.

LEFTWARD TENDENCIES

Left tendencies signify introversion, the inner life, meditation, introspection, isolation, passiveness, self-knowledge, retention of unresolved inner conflicts. The more strongly you are influenced by the past, the more frequent will be your leftward tendencies.

Positive Example	Description	Indication
ƒ ∂ aⅆ that	In upper zone.	Meditation, reflection, intellectual self-dependence.
cin m	In middle zone.	Connection with the past, independence.
age	In lower zone.	Instinctive apperception of the past.

Negative Example	Description	Indication
ƒ ∂ aⅆ that	In upper zone.	Introspection, withdrawal, preoccupation with past memories and imagination, brooding over repressed thoughts.
𝒪𝓃	In upper zone, with curls, embellishments and exaggerations.	Mentally ill.
cin m	In middle zone.	Selfish, egotistic.
y	In lower zone, with wide, large loops.	Erotic fantasy.
y	With angular lower loops.	Irritability.
ð ð ð	With twisted or distorted lower loops.	Self-love, narcissism, inversion of the libido.
ƒ ð ƒ	Lower loops insecurely pressed to the left and distorted.	Homosexuality.

Base Line Direction

The base line is the line real or assumed upon which the letters are written and progress to the right on the paper. Since the direction of the base line indicates the emotions, feelings and physical condition at the time when the script was written, one specimen of writing is not always sufficient to determine whether the line is variable or characteristic. For example, a descending line may be caused by sudden fatigue but also by depression of longer duration. However, if a study of other features of the writing shows a normal balanced condition, it indicates fatigue, illness or stress following a loss or shock.

As the base line varies, so does the control of the emotions. Hence, few people can maintain an almost straight base line because it takes quite an amount of steadfastness, equanimity and self-discipline to continuously maintain a level base line.

The base line can be straight (even), wavering, irregular, ascending, descending, convex, concave; it can show ascending steps and descending steps.

When in doubt whether a base line is straight, turn the page upside down or trace a straight line across the page. This gives a clear indication whether the line is straight or wavering.

Positive Example	Description	Indication
The use of a large and	A straight, even, or level base line without using lined paper.	Stable, purposeful, good balance, self-control, reason rules the emotions, steadfast, sincere, honest, straightforward, reliable, perseveres in an aim or goal and follows through in an undertaking.

if it was found

Slightly upward.

Ambitious, hopeful, optimistic, enthusiastic; initiative, mental activity; lively, not easily discouraged. Can smile in the face of defeat.

from a distance

Extremely upward.

Exuberant, elation, enthusiastic, zeal, imaginative; but being overly ambitious, may overshoot the goal and be impractical. A pushing body and spirit.

I was not quite

Concave, dips in the middle.

Initial self-distrust and pessimism which steadily gains courage to act, having once begun a task, finishes it. Successful fight against a pessimistic attitude. (This cautious working manner is adopted by people whose goals are high and who want to explore them fully before undertaking to achieve them.)

A larger problem.

Wavering lines, with good form; level, rhythmic.

Versatility and diplomacy.

Negative Example	Description	Indication

habitual with

Straight base line, with variations of letter forms.

Individual not calm or composed but able to discipline self to maintain attitude of calmness.

What would he

Slightly downward.

Despondency or languidness which may be the outcome of bodily fatigue and exhaustion. Troubled, worrying, indecisive, lacking in ambition.

Handwriting	Direction	Traits
A young man of	Downward.	Despondent, pessimistic, discouraged, moody, apathetic, melancholic; ailing health, lacking in mental alertness.
Did he go there	Extremely downward.	Serious or dangerous depression.
Some other way.	Wavering (uneven) or sinuous.	Instability, unsteady working habits, nervousness, moody, inconsistent, weather-vane personality, insincere, unreliable; disappointment in life.
and was at my	Irregular or varying (going in different directions).	Impressionable, changeable moods, instability, fickleness, vacillating indecision, nervousness, lack of mental control and discipline.
like the one you	Convex or arched.	Zeal and ambition, but no perseverance. Makes a good start with ambition and self-confidence but because of little stamina and energy loses interest and gives up before aim is reached. Periodic change between enthusiasm and sinking spirits.

Connections and Disconnections

When we learn how to write, we are instructed to write cursively, that is, to connect all the letters in a word; but later in life we may deviate in varying degrees from this method. While some of us will continue to connect all the letters in a word, others will produce their own individual method of connections.

If you will observe your writing carefully, you will see that you connect one letter to another by a movement to the right in an upward direction and a disconnection is mainly caused by the omission of the upstrokes which connect one letter to another. When you lift your hand unconsciously and omit the upstroke, you pause to permit a flash of intuition to enter.

The writers of connected and disconnected writings are completely different in mental processes, attitudes and outlook on life.

CONNECTED WRITING

If you connect your letters in a word, writing the word solidly from beginning to end, you think and reason logically. You are a deductive thinker who thinks from cause to effect. You have an instinct for relatedness to people and things, and experience no difficulty in establishing social relationships, and you will be better in the practical world than an intuitive person. However, you will be constructive rather than creative.

Connected writing implies a logical mind and logical reasoning that springs from a continuity of thought. Ideas will be closely related to each other. Connected writing symbolizes adaptability and has three aspects, the practical, theoretical and moral. When at least five letters are written in one continuing stroke, the script is considered connected. Interruptions for the application of *i* dots and *t* bars do not count as such.

Positive Example	Description	Indication
simple matters	All letters connected in a word.	Logical reasoning, deductive, abstract and systematic thinking, adaptability, planning, steadiness in work, sociable, practical, continuity and fluency of thought.

Example	Description	Indication
A great man in history	With clear spacing of words and lines, above-average form-level.	Logical thought, great intelligence, power of deduction, accurate mind.
for long and	Complete words connected to each other with literary *g* and *d* and reverse *f*.	Able to speak and write effortlessly; literary talent, quick fluid thought.
which are not a	Complete words connected to each other.	Exceptionally clever mind, keen logical faculties for discovering solutions to difficult problems, thorough, intelligent, fluidity of thought, good executive; also chessboard, political and military strategist.
it is time	With light pressure, high *i* dots and *t* bar.	Though logical there are flashes of intuition which are not trusted because reasons must be found for everything.
Taking familiar	Moderately connected.	Memory for facts.
As quick as possible	With quick writing, clear spacing.	Memory for logical connections.
another time to arrange a	With vertical slant, small writing, clear spacing.	Intelligent, deductive thinker, penetrative in making decisions; sentiment does not sway decisions, good resistance. Usually found in the writing of judges and lawyers.

Negative Example	Description	Indication
simple matters	All letters connected.	Lack of creativeness, originality, and intuition; difficult to convince once mind is made up; one-track mind, poverty of ideas, overadaptability, tendency to talkativeness and familiarity.

W 1641886

which are nota   Words connected.   Can be stubborn, obstinate and opinionated, stickler for principles, conservative.

For a long period of   With below-average form level.   Obedience to routine, materialistic tendency, deduction pushed to extreme.

DISCONNECTED WRITING

If you separate your letters in your words, you are intuitive, you are an inductive thinker who jumps from cause to effect without traveling the longer and slower road of reason and deduction which a logical person must follow. In other words, you have quick perception of relationships without apparent meditation; you often seem to get surprising conclusions out of the depths of your subconscious mind. You will be full of ideas which emerge separately without regard to the others or the possibility of a connection. However, you will be poor in cooperation and adaptation, find it difficult to establish contacts, and feel isolated.

The completely intuitive person is rare but such intuition can be a liability. A person with too much theory and too many visionary ideas does not possess enough logic or reason to enable him to put them into effect. The more intuitive you are, the more likely you are to jump to conclusions.

When intuition and logic (connectedness and disconnectedness) are evenly balanced or nearly so in a person's writing, he is able to take the theory which intuition gives him and work it out practically with his logic and reason. His intuition speeds his perception and gives him resourcefulness in sudden and unexpected emergencies.

While in its positive aspect intuition is considered one of the most important and precious qualities of the human consciousness (when it is latent and unused, as it is in many people, it leaves them incomplete in their development), in its negative aspect it indicates weakness of will and the incapacity to be consistently practical, moral, and intellectual.

When less than four letters are written in one continuing stroke, the writing is considered disconnected.

Positive Example	Description	Indication
Greetings on your birthday	With above-average form level.	Intuitive mind, ability to sense situations before they happen, perceptive, analytical, intellectual, observant, emotionally sensitive, versatile, original, sharp imagination, reflection before action, idea can germinate, insight. Found in the writing of artists.
certain interesting characters	Combination of connected and disconnected writing (mixed connections), evenly balanced.	Versatile, adaptable, flexible, can work theory out practically, combines logic and intuition in making decisions. (Dominant connection determines dominant trait.)

Negative Example	Description	Indication
As for what was done is	All letters in a word disconnected.	Uncooperative, unsociable, does not care to adapt or conform in ways expected of the individual, favors intuition over logic, jumps too quickly to conclusion without benefit of reasoning; thinking often disconnected and jerky, lack of concentration, weak willpower, incapacity to be consistently practical or moral, often erratic, hasty, unorganized, obsessed by details.

under the circumstances	Most letters in a word disconnected.	Unsociable, eccentric, egotistic, whimsical, inconsistent, moody, restless when dreams do not materialize, lacks adaptability, and logical reasoning, shy, selfish, avaricious.
handwriting disclosed	Combination of connected and disconnected writing, mixed connections.	Intuition and logic often set up indecision, unnecessary tension and irritability over trifles; sometimes torn between reason and intuition. Some instability, strong likes and dislikes, impatience. Found in creative writers, inventors, those independent in thought, individualists, unconventional; self-reliance, tactfulness, ideas can germinate, emotionally sensitive, having musical talent. Independent, quick grasp.
for as what could be done	All letters disconnected.	Likes to deal with ideas, unique and discrete; creative intellect, imagination, often filled with new concepts which he wants to execute immediately. Individualistic, intuitive, self-reliant. Found in writing of poets and artists.
gentleman of leisure is to	Some letters disconnected.	Inventive, "idea man," critical observer and examiner, artistic and intuitive thinker, individualistic, witty, imaginative.
take a little of the cake	All letters disconnected, with small writing.	Highly sensitive, introspective, imaginative.
understand the numbers that	Some letters disconnected, with light pressure.	Natural memory and receptivity.

Take a while for large	First letter stands apart while the rest of the writing is connected.	Caution, will pause before acting (looks before he leaps); observant, quick emotional changes, sensitivity, may have good reasoning and creativity but may lack concentration.
Family of seven	Disconnected writing in below-average form level.	Illogical mind, inability to focus thoughts sequentially; impractical.
in the first line below a	Disconnected, with slow, lean writing, small size.	Lack of faculty of adjustment, poor memory.
a long way to go from	With large lower loops hitting into line below, entangled.	Intuition leads the individual astray because judgment is faulty due to superficial evidence.
making them	With narrow arcade letters and left slant.	Fear of life and does not face responsibilities.
what of the day	With angular connections.	Central conflict within the individual.
promises it	With garland writing.	Limited adaptability due to heavy-heartedness.
wh at *a ct i on*	Large irregular gaps between letters.	Overreacts to irritation from the outside, psychic (mental) disturbance.
	Structure of writing is dissolved; without form rather than disconnected.	Mental imbalance or mental disturbance, nervous disease, acute negative qualities.
WISHES TO SEE HIM WHENEVER	Typescript (manuscript writing), if not used professionally.	Not considered disconnected writing since it is a copying of print. Used by people who hide their own weaknesses behind the motionless wall of printed letters.

The Three Zones

Handwriting consists of three zones, upper, middle and lower. They reveal our attitudes towards life.

ZONES							CHARACTER
	UPPER			SUPEREGO	UPPER LOOPS	MIND	
	MIDDLE	*I go to a*		EGO	SMALL LETTERS	SOUL	
	LOWER			ID	LOWER LOOPS	BODY	
		SUBCONSCIOUS					

The upper zone reveals the conscience, the intellectual, philosophical, spiritual and ethical interests, imaginative powers, creative ideas and sometimes religious aspirations.

The middle zone is the social zone and reveals the conscious, practical and unimaginative daily life. Here are expressed your likes, dislikes, habits, emotional attitudes and reactions, and adaptability to reality and to everyday activities. The middle zone is the essential and central part of the writing, yet it is the most inconspicuous part of it.

The lower zone reveals the subconscious, material wants, business interests, instinctual and physical life, sensuality and sex drives.

A balance between the three zones indicates a balanced and integrated person and an equilibrium of interest in the three zones. A disproportion, such as an exaggeration of a zone, shows the direction in which the interest is exaggerated at the expense of the other zones. This lack of symmetry reveals a lack of inner balance and development.

PREPONDERANCE OF THE UPPER ZONE

Positive Example	*Description*	*Indication*
pliable	With high upper loops, pointed at the top, and high *i* dots.	An intellectual with an active imagination and idealistic, philosophic or religious interests.
fling	Emphasis on upper zone, short lower loops.	Enthusiasm, idealism, active imagination, intellectuality, spiritual temperament, conscious emphasis on freedom, determination and independence, ambition, abstract thinker.

Negative Example	*Description*	*Indication*
fling	Emphasis on upper zone, short lower loops.	Lack of roots and of objectivity; flightiness, exaltation, fickleness, superficiality (in social and value relations).
Mel	Emphasis on upper loops with exaggerated and bizarre flourishes.	Preoccupation with illusions and dreams, mental aberrations, unbalanced fantasies of the insane.
building	Upper zone substantial in size, middle zone neglected.	Not well integrated, unsure of emotional reactions to daily living because of inattention to own emotional needs; disregards the need for their expression.

PREPONDERANCE OF THE MIDDLE ZONE

Positive Example	Description	Indication
mostly	Emphasis on the middle zone with upper and lower loops short.	Practical, realistic, doesn't spend time in dreaming, not influenced by fantasies. Has no impelling sex drive; simple, unpretentious, modest, mature.
Mr.	Middle zone letters raised into the upper zone.	Preoccupation with intellectual and spiritual life, desire for creative thinking, fertile imagination.

Negative Example	Description	Indication
mostly	Emphasis on middle zone; lower and upper zone short.	Dislikes change or exertion, no taste for striving, expansion or enterprise, narrow range of interest.
halting	Large middle zone, upper zone dwarfed.	Too concerned with social relations at expense of intellectual and spiritual interests.
greatly	Large middle zone, short lower lengths.	Too much interest in social relations and not sufficiently concerned with material demands and instincts.
get two or	Overextended middle zone.	Concerned with self, self-centered, overemphasizes the ego, subjective in outlook, egocentric.
more men were in	Large middle zone with rigid letters of stereotyped regularity.	Schizoid personality.

good help for

Emphasis on middle
and lower zone,
upper zone
undeveloped.

Lacks imagination, ideals,
intelligence and ambition. No
real pride or ethics,
materialistic.

PREPONDERANCE OF THE LOWER ZONE

Positive Example	Description	Indication
flying trip	Large, long, emphasized lower zone, longer than upper zone.	Physically active, practical, and technical inclinations, earthiness, active imagination, warmth, thoroughness, conscious emphasis on responsibility, necessity and obligation.
flags fly	Excessively long lower loops, short upper loops, proportion unbalanced.	Strongly attached to the earth, at home in practical and material spheres based on instinctual feelings; observant, thorough.

Negative Example	Description	Indication
flying trip	Large, long, emphasized lower zone, longer than upper zone.	Materialism, sensuality, voraciousness, greed, clumsiness, pedestrianism.
flags fly	Excessively long lower loops, proportion unbalanced.	Lacking spiritual and intellectual agility, slow thinking, root bound, clumsy, disposed to brooding, holds on to whatever was once grasped.

| *young for* | Large, long, emphasized, inflated loops in lower zone, with heavy pressure | Sensualist, strong sex drive, sex dreams, ambition for material success and worth, greed, voraciousness. |

Spacing

Writing is not only a means of communication but a movement in space. The sheet of paper represents the world in which you find yourself; if your writing shows well-balanced spacing, you are able to adapt to the circumstances at your disposal. Marked irregularity in the size of spacing indicates disorder and lack of rhythm.

Enterprising organizers, scholars and scientists will show good spacing between the lines and words, while the more imaginative and intuitive person will be inclined to a less clear spacing in his writing. The spacing of words and lines is symbolic of your organizational and surveying abilities, your reflection, whether you are orderly or disorderly, tolerant or intolerant, and whether your thinking is clear or muddled.

Clear spacing between words does not necessarily coincide with a clear distance between the lines.

SPACING BETWEEN WORDS

Spacing between words is nondeliberate. Even very sensitive people have no idea whether or not they leave spaces between the words or whether they are large or small.

Positive Example	Description	Indication
for two of a	Sizable and even.	Orderly, well-organized, clear judgment and thinking, interest in literature, music, philosophic turn of mind, deep feeling, critical, firmly rooted convictions, introverted.
if one is in	Wide.	Generous, courageous, independent.
put a small one	Small, even, good form level.	Activity, reasonableness; talkative, uncritical, extroverted, self-confident, well-balanced.

Negative Example	Description	Indication
for a day	Wide.	Considerable degree of reserve, caution and shyness.
for a time	Too wide.	Extravagance, love of luxury, audacity, affectation.
if he had	Extremely wide gaps between words.	Fear of people, inhibition, tendency to be isolated from environment either socially or psychologically, difficulty in communicating with others.
had she done	Too wide, with small writing.	Lonesome, critical observer.
its a good way to	Uneven.	Never learned to make the most of his natural talents.
its a good way to	Sizable, uneven, good form level.	Critical way of thinking and reasoning, trickiness.
after he left a	Sizable, uneven, inferior form level.	Indecision, inability to think clearly.
come along to the	Small, uneven.	Talkative, gullible, inharmonious personality.

it is quite bigfor	Spacing at beginning of line ample but ends up squeezed or distorted.	Lack of planning, precaution and precision.
theyaresobigthathe	Too narrow, crowded; words too close together.	Lack of reserve. Does not keep his distance nor care for privacy, wants human contact; insecure ego, impulsive, acquisitive and frugal.
The word to wise is	Large spacing between words, insufficient spacing between lines.	Clarity only for short distance.
you and he	Large writing, narrow word spacing.	Lack of objectivity and impartiality.

SPACING BETWEEN LINES

Spacing between lines is one of the features that can be seen and analyzed at first sight or even from afar. When the area of writing space is sufficient, it is easy to separate the lines; even when it is limited, a clear-minded person will still allow for balanced spacing between lines, though this may mean reducing the size of his normal writing.

Spacing between lines reflects your mental ability and clear objective thinking. Irregularity of the line spacing shows lack of willpower. Confused spacing reveals a subjective mind, clear spacing an objective mind.

The interval between lines of writing can be too wide, wide, narrow, too narrow, or small and irregular.

Positive Example	Description	Indication
They kept them	Wide.	Clear objective thinking, analytical mind, good manners, desire for cleanliness, consideration, makes good teacher, organizer and executive, strives for logical certainty.
in good order		
How tall was		
the tree he cut		
down near the	Equidistant.	Strong sense of justice.

Negative Example	Description	Indication
They kept them	Wide.	Lacks spontaneity.
in good order		
How many miles	Too wide.	Incoherent, weak-minded; disorganized thinking, imminent mental derangement.
is it to the		
When Mary came home she found the house tidy	Small spaces with absence of upper margins.	Lack of self-reliance and an anxious holding on to environmental positions already secured.
It was too far for John to go so they took a bus to the store	Too narrow or crowded, lines entangle.	Cannot survey a situation; hasty decisions, lack of reserve and determination; cannot see things as they are.
This boy was quite tall for his age but his sister was somewhat shorter	Irregular.	Illogical mind, poor judgment and adjustment, careless, not methodical, lack of willpower.
Why did he go there, in the first place	Poor spacing, connected and broad writing, lines entangled.	Disorganized, unable to plan thought and action.

Mary and John put out their	Lines overlap, lower zone descends into next line.	Lack of inhibitions, unable to control sexual impulse, preoccupied with instinctual life.
Many knew why Helga went to New York	Lower loops crowd capitals while middle zone remains clear.	Capable of managing routine, incapable of thinking and proper emotional life, loses head in an emergency.
Enjoy your trip to the island	Lower loops overlong, reach into upper zone of following line.	Confused emotions in which unfulfilled love and sex life are transformed to the realm of the imagination. Various spheres, the intellectual, emotional and instinctual, are mixed up.

SPACING BETWEEN WORDS AND LINES

A well-spaced script (between lines and words) indicates the writer's culture, intelligence, quick clear understanding and liberality. Crowded spacing in a script implies thrift or stinginess.

Positive Example	Description	Indication
Imagine how this man would take	Wide, clear and even, above-average form level.	Clarity of thought, objective mind, ability to separate thoughts, good judgment, emotional stability, reliability, intelligence above average.
A well earned day off from	Wide.	Self-confidence, determination; liberal, orderly thinking, social, impatient.
A good time was had by	Well-spaced, full, quick, large writing.	Gifted or superior person.

Negative Example	Description	Indication
It is for us to be	Too wide, with large script.	Lavish, inconsiderate; isolation, incoherence.

[handwriting sample]	Too narrow, lack of spacing.	Lack of objectivity, intolerance; thrifty, confused, disorganized.
[handwriting sample]	Words and lines entangled.	Conflict of ideas, confused mind, disorder, lacks poise, unreliable; mental disturbance, false judgment, inferiority, irritability.
[handwriting sample]	Irregular or uneven, varied slant and size.	Emotionally unstable, moody, temperamental and weak-willed.
[handwriting sample]	Poor or insufficient, broad writing, lines entangled.	Disorganized, unable to plan thought and action.
[handwriting sample]	No spacing or nearly none.	Set ideas, intolerant, reserved, cautious, economical.
[handwriting sample]	Words evenly spaced, lines unevenly spaced.	Not well balanced; and weak. Has both positive and negative traits; can be self-assured and tolerant, but also restless and inconsistent.
[handwriting sample]	Increased regularity, insufficient spacing.	

Regularity and Irregularity

As a human being cannot produce absolute regularity in his handwriting, the handwriting movement can be described as having a greater or lesser regularity.

Look at your handwriting to get a general impression of this dominant feature. Does it look well-balanced?

1. Are all your letters approximately equal in size, height and width?

2. Is the slant constant?
3. Is the base line straight?
4. Is the spacing between lines and words even and clear?

If you see these signs in your handwriting, it is considered regular writing. If these four features vary or change considerably, the writing is irregular.

REGULARITY

Regular writing requires a certain amount of discipline (self-control) and concentration forced by the intellect and will. It is a sign of regularity of mind and conduct, i.e., a good willpower.

Positive Example	Description	Indication
Take part of the lid	According to the four features required for regularity.	Willpower, control and discipline, well balanced, sense of harmony, capacity for work and concentration, persevering, methodical, consistency, orderly, reliable, physical resistance, poise.
A good thing for Henry	With quick writing and original letter forms.	Self-control, willpower, firmness, constancy, responsibility and persistence.
HE will get full value	With strong pressure, large and original forms.	Strong willpower which disciplines and balances natural impulses.

Negative Example	Description	Indication
One day he will be at	Regular.	Lack of excitability and capacity to change, sometimes pedantry and monotony, dullness, unimpressionability.

Positive Example	Description	Indication
can he do this at	With angularity.	Little adaptability to circumstances; rigidity of feeling, inelasticity, compulsiveness.
all of a sudden	In slow writing with below-average form level.	Obedience, lack of feeling and originality, indifference or mechanicalness.
for the men with brawn	Tendencies to rigid regularity.	Often leads to compulsive behavior; schizoid personality.
Phil and I were in a	In copybook style.	Lack of vitality, personality and imagination.

IRREGULARITY

In irregular writing, the emotions and spontaneity prevail or are stronger than the willpower to discipline them. Irregular writing has opposite qualities to regularity.

Positive Example	Description	Indication
Great for a likeness	With individual letter forms.	An artist or a creative mind. Sensitiveness, imagination, warmth, impressionable, vivacious, emotional.

Negative Example	Description	Indication
you should take as many	Irregularity.	Lack of willpower, undisciplined, imbalanced, changeable and variable moods, nervousness, lack of steadiness, untidiness, many-sided interests, lack of planning, purpose, and concentration, easily influenced, undirected energies; feelings and impulses stronger than the will to direct them to a desired goal; tossed about by the emotions, conflict as to work and discipline, a weak character.
for two places at	With uneven pressure.	Instability of emotions, inconsistency of character.
are many of the tops	With slow, banal writing.	Lack of energy, balance and discipline.

Size

The size of the script symbolizes your estimate of yourself and your role in life. It is a gauge of your intellect, ability to concentrate and aptness for detail. It is determined by the size of the small letters (middle zone). The size of these letters can be small, very small, medium, large or very large. The size is measured vertically, which means the actual height of the letter.

A medium height is about one-eighth inch and is the school model. If your letters are larger than the school model, they are considered large. If smaller, they are considered small or very small. The height of small letters is subject to great changeableness or variation. Only people of very stable disposition with never-changing self-confidence are able to maintain the same height in the middle zone.

Positive Example	Description	Indication
market	Medium size.	Adaptable, conforming, unassuming, moderate, reasonable, practical; of average tastes, ideas and desires.
others	Large size, good form level.	Outgoing, enterprising, spontaneous, animated; pride, generosity, interest in big plans and issues, organizing ability.
rated	Very large.	Physically active, social; zeal, animation, vivacity.
degree	Small.	Good mind and memory, intelligent, good concentration, realistic, observant, analytical, attention to detail, modest, accurate, usually scientific.
very good	Very small.	High degree of concentration, scholastic, intellectual, introspective, reserved, unassuming, modest, methodical. Capable of doing meticulous work, channels energy into thinking rather than action. Scientist.
balanced	Letters all the same size, clear, legible.	Balanced evaluation of the things that interest you. Subconscious in harmony with the conscious mind, communicates clearly, hides nothing, consistent person, conscientious.

variations	Variations of letters on an even base line.	Natural versatility, sensitivity, speedy, impatient, inconsistent.
angle	Extremely large in angular script.	Animation, zeal, enthusiasm, vivacity, high spirits, entertaining talker, insists upon having own way.
increasing	Increasing size of letters.	Conscientious, high ethical values, straightforward, honest.
decreasing	Decreasing size of letters.	Tact, reserve.

Negative Example	Description	Indication
rated	Very large size.	Excessive pride, pretentiousness, physically active, finds it difficult to concentrate, can't stay long on one task, likes to be seen and heard, likes the grandiose and luxurious, extravagant in everything, restless, materialistic, likes to be admired.
others	Large.	Restless, impatient, bored by details, lack of concentration. Poor observer, hard to satisfy. Conceit, arrogance; generalizes.
degree	Small.	Lack of self-confidence, inferiority feelings, overscrupulous.
busy all day with	Very small, with below-average form level.	Petty exactitude, cannot distinguish between what is important and what is not.
allowing	Very small with angularity and narrowness.	Inferiority complex, introvert, narrow-minded.

alternating	Variations of size in small, medium and large script with an uneven base line.	Inconsistent, impatient, immature. Likes variety. Thoughtless, indecisive, controlled by feelings, unreliable.
variations	Variations of letters with even base line.	Inconsistency, can be influenced.
general	Small letters *e* and *r* written larger in proportion to small letters.	Preoccupation with self-importance and possibly fond of material things; snobbishness.
increasing	Increasing size of letters.	Tendency to blurt things out impetuously and impulsively, overcoming caution. Naive honesty. Conscientious, easily imposed upon.
decreasing	Decreasing size of letters.	Diplomacy, shrewdness in dealing with others, does not tell everything that is on his mind.
entirely too small	So small that it needs to be examined by a magnifying glass.	Fear, indecision, inhibition. Resembles a tightly wound watch that is apt to snap under pressure; energies go to brain, everything intellectualized. Emotions drained of their warmth. Introspective, not apt to have close friends.
slanting	Slurred small letters.	Impatient with details, secretive, evasive.

Speed or Tempo

Every person has his own basic tempo which is set for him by his innate nervous system. Physiological studies have shown that the tempo of thinking and writing are intimately correlated. Experiments have substantiated that it is the sweep of ideas which carries the writing along and ultimately determines speed.

Speed in writing, like speed in any other function, increases with practice. When we first learn to write, the tempo is painstakingly slow, but it increases until we attain automatized fluency in adulthood. Speed expresses the speed of our reactions, whether we are apt to be quick or deliberate, hasty or sluggish in action, thought, emotional response and social relations. When a change of emotion occurs while writing, the writer's normal speed will be changed as shown by stops, hasty strokes or in leftward strokes.

FAST TEMPO

The following features indicate fast tempo:

1. Strokes smoothly and firmly made.
2. *i* dots and periods in the form of commas.
3. *i* dots and *t* bars omitted or placed to the right and elongated.
4. Increased tendency to the rightward slant, no change of direction.
5. Ascending lines.
6. Wide script.
7. Increased leftward margin.
8. Connected writing.
9. Simplification.

10. Garland or thready connections.
11. Avoidance of covering strokes.
12. Abbreviation of words.
13. Incompletion of last letters of words.
14. Prolonged ending strokes.
15. Irregularity.
16. Good distribution of spaces.
17. Neglect of detail.
18. Pressure light or medium.
19. Short beginning strokes.
20. Long stems.
21. Long slim loops.

Positive Example	*Description*	*Indication*
He thinks quickly	Fast writing.	Spontaneous, naturalness of expression, vivaciousness, fast in action and reaction, quick mental grasp, alert, executes ideas with speed, adaptable, initiative; has better chance of success in a competitive society than the slow writer. Extrovert.
I wish it was in there	Quick, large, well-connected, rightward slant, *i* dots ahead with large left margin.	An active mind, open to development and progress, emotional expansiveness.
They were first to	Quick, rhythmic, well-spaced, large, full script.	Talented and gifted person.
would you be	With rightward slant.	Extrovert, one who enjoys meeting people and finds satisfaction outside of himself.

Negative Example	Description	Indication
what should he	Quick or speedy.	Superficial, lack of steadiness, flighty, rash, instability, irritability, impulsive.
at last she is coming home	Hasty writing, too quick.	Impulsive, impatient, restless, unable to keep thoughts on one subject without difficulty, lack of discipline.
when would he be if she put	Hasty with irregularity.	Lack of control.

SLOW TEMPO

Slow tempo symbolizes low energy and caution. It is determined by the following:

1. *i* dots and *t* bars omitted or placed to the left.
2. *i* dots exact, and in the center.
3. Leftward slant and predominance of leftward tendencies.
4. Descending lines.
5. Narrow writing.
6. Decreased leftward margin as it descends on the page.
7. Disconnected writing.
8. Ornamentation.
9. Angular or arcade connections.
10. Covering or concealing strokes.
11. Completion of final letters of words.
12. Lack of smoothness in strokes.
13. Poor distribution of spaces.
14. Attention to detail.
15. Shortened end strokes, clipped or curled, or left-turned.
16. Left margin narrowing as it proceeds down the page.
17. Even left margin.

18. Carefully made initial strokes.
19. Touched-up writing.
20. Size very large or very small.
21. Broken or jerky letters.
22. Writing too uniform, regular and monotonous.
23. Copybook writing.
24. Vertical writing (slant).
25. Change of direction after breaks in words.
26. Pasty, smeary writing or blotchy ovals.

Positive Example	Description	Indication
are you in first	Slow.	Slow in action and reaction, cautious, careful, steady, passive, ponders before leaping. Introvert. Low energy, slow mind.
A full measure	Slow, regular, original, rhythmic, pasty and disconnected writing.	Capacity for thoughtful observation and meditation, desire for beauty.

Negative Example	Description	Indication
one time	Slow, with uniform writing.	Lazy, inertia, dislikes physical exertion.
it is my right	Slow, with left slant and arcade connection.	Calculating; schemers who hide their purposes.
one day a	Slow and dilatory.	Melancholic.
an afternoon	Slow, rigid and regular.	Symbol of deceit.
they will	Slow, with weak pressure.	Weakness and apathy.
if he will do it	Slow, leftward, narrow, exact dotting of *i*.	Hesitation. procrastination.

MEDIUM SPEED

Positive Example	Description	Indication
a good book	Medium tempo.	Average intelligence and energy.

Margins

Margins are the spaces on the top, bottom, left side and right side which form the body of the writing on the writing sheet. They govern the arrangement of the rows of words on the paper, automatically producing the various margins which provide an overall look at the script and you. The margins you make and where you begin mostly indicate your aesthetic taste, your tendency to thrift or extravagance, and your ability to plan and follow through on tasks.

The left-hand margin symbolizes the past and the self and is the starting point. The right-hand margin symbolizes the future and the world and represents the goal. When the left- and right-hand margins conflict in width or are different, there is a conflict between generosity and thrift. Neurotics and some criminals have a compulsion not to write close to the right-hand margin and will cross this margin with a horizontal stroke.

The upper margin has little significance. If it is large, you express a respect toward the addressee; it is usually used in conventional letters. Its lack reveals a lack of respect and obtrusiveness.

Lack of a lower margin is not instinctively noticed. The writer concentrates on communication. A wide lower margin expresses aesthetic feeling and a generous attitude toward material things.

Other features in the handwriting will have to be considered in making an analysis of a handwriting, but they generally corroborate the margin findings.

Legibility and Illegibility

Legibility and illegibility are measures of the writer's sense of purposefulness, his intentions, plans, agreeability and social cooperation.

LEGIBILITY

Writing is a means of communication with others, and the necessity for legibility is self-evident; we are taught to write legibly. Therefore, if a person writes legibly, we assume that he wants to be understood. One who does work requiring meticulous detail is likely to write with a clear, uniform script.

Certain mental and physical disorders and nervousness are likely to nullify the most serious attempts to write legibly. However, since there are certain mental disorders which produce painstakingly legible writing, we must understand the whole before we can understand the parts.

Positive Example	Description	Indication
Some of the good qualities	With clear spaces between lines and words, above-average form level.	Wants clear communication and understanding with others; sincere, open character, honest, straightforward, purposefulness, high intelligence, clear thinking, cooperative, sociable, conscientious, self-disciplined. Carefulness in detail.
can you and John	With average form level.	Slow but accurate thinker.

Negative Example	Description	Indication
A place in the country	Impressively and meticulously legible in a model penmanship. Also in calligraphic script.	The "wolf in sheep's clothing" who wants to appear open but is dishonest and deceptive; hides something to avoid detection. Also shows immaturity, living in a narrow world.

ILLEGIBILITY

In general, illegibility is a negative sign, although intellectuals and artists sometimes write illegibly. The uneducated and illiterate generally write illegibly, though education itself does not necessarily result in legible writing.

The writer of an illegible hand is inconsiderate of those who must try to read it, and there may be a deep psychological reason for guilt or an inability to adjust to ordinary conventions and social customs.

Usually in illegible writing, the pressure tends to be muddy, pasty or blurred to make it impossible for the reader to find out the writer. Forms of letters become indistinct or slurred, letters confused; unimportant letters are exaggerated with loose and threadlike connections, often cramped and poorly spaced.

Positive Example	Description	Indication
our michaov will la n for	With good form level.	Secretiveness, confidential, desire to be individualistic and for freedom of action; adaptable, intuitive, imaginative, reservedness, able to understand others, maturity.

Negative Example	Description	Indication
ini wichowc will lo m fo	With good form level.	Carelessness, uncooperative, inconsiderate, bad manners, insincerity, unpunctuality, suspicion, mistrust, neurotic fear, arrogance, confused state of mind. Indolence.
graceful disgrac	With above-average form level.	Aesthetic taste, artistry, nervousness, unlimited imagination, impatience with routine, carelessness, nonconformity, disorder.
for no good ancestors	With below-average form level.	Confusion, inhibition, secrecy, crudeness, indecision.
come	Conscious or unconscious illegibility, or retouching.	Does not want to reveal actual self clearly and definitely, wants to confuse and mislead. This reveals deceit and untruthfulness.
many things	Many letters slurred.	Evasiveness, does not want to reveal self though he may pretend to do so. Always remains a mystery in some respect. He can talk a good deal but one never really knows him.

Width and Narrowness

Since width or narrowness of a script is seen from the aspect of a left or right movement and is restricted to the middle zone, it reveals one's adjustment to everyday life.

WIDE WRITING

Width of writing is an outward movement to the world, away from the ego or the person. It produces a horizontal effect, the upstrokes are emphasized and there is a rightward movement originating from an unrestricted movement of the hand. It signifies extroversion, enterprise and sociability. It indicates a lack of constraint and concerns the I-to-you relationship.

A wide script is one in which the distance between the downstrokes of a letter is larger than the height. It is called primary width. Secondary width is between two or more letters.

Positive Example	Description	Indication
imagine	With heavy pressure.	Spontaneity, drive, sociability, frankness, liberality, courage, striving, goal-mindedness, active, ambition, expansion.
primary	With light pressure.	Imagination and vision, impressionability, generosity, simplicity.
hamper	With vertical slant and a few tendencies to the left.	A balanced person.

Negative Example	Description	Indication
playing	With garlands and rhythmic pacing.	Broad-mindedness; friendly.
imagine	With heavy pressure.	Lack of self-control, reserve and discipline; lack of economy. Tactless, rashness, impatient, inconsiderateness, gregariousness, careless.
primary	With light pressure.	Superficiality, haste, impatience, prodigality, carelessness.
flame	With right slant.	Prodigality, easily influenced, not properly anchored to self, depends on outside world.
horn	Extravagantly wide letters.	Claims for space and significance.
if he is in for a	Very wide, large spaces between words, three words on line, broad margin at left, slant rightward.	Spendthrift inclinations, possible gambler, careless, impatient, extroverting too much, unable to regulate and control feelings toward others and properly arrange time and money, dissipates energies. Not sufficiently rooted in self.
way	With large writing.	Expansive, needs an audience.
will he be at my	With left slant.	Sociability combined with suspicion. A sociable disposition that has learned to be cautious and clever.
what can he do away from	With narrow spacing, irregularity, narrowing margins.	Inconsiderate, tactless, talkative.
early in frost	Spacing between letters (primary width) wide, but distance between downstrokes (secondary width) is narrow.	A contradiction here. Writer is effective in outward activities (social) but inhibited in emotional expression; wants to appear more natural and generous than he really is.

NARROW WRITING

A narrow script is an inward movement to the ego, the writer himself. It produces a vertical movement, with downstrokes emphasized, and is also a leftward movement. Narrow writing signifies introversion, constriction, shyness, economy or stinginess. Hypocrites and forgers choose a narrow script.

A narrow script is one in which the distance between the downstrokes is less than the height.

Positive Example	Description	Indication
money for	With heavy pressure.	Self-control, reserve, tactful, economy, reason, moderation.
also coming	With light pressure.	Caution, modesty, contentment.
now is the	With regular writing.	Capacity for work and endurance, will not waste money or emotions.

Negative Example	Description	Indication
a very good	With heavy pressure.	Overcautious, self-contained, inhibited, distrust, calculation, jealousy, avarice, negativism, deceitfulness, reluctance to give, anxiety.
time for	With light pressure.	Timidity, distrust, anxiety, neurotic inhibition, narrow views, fear of life.
grand piano	Vertical slant, and many breaks.	Greedy person.
one of those	With small, irregular and slow writing.	Pedantry, intolerance.
money in	With angularity.	Discipline.

Positive Example	Description	Indication
after the party	Extreme narrowness.	Timidity, inhibition, anxiousness, discouragement, egocentricity; suspicious, petty, uncertainty, torn by inner conflicts, contradictory feelings.
from two places en the	Extremely narrow with small, slow, irregular writing. Missing end strokes.	Meanness.
planted	Narrowness to the extent that downstrokes cover the upstrokes.	Severe constraint, may be due to psychological motives, egocentric speculation and lack of uprightness.
have you	Upright slant, restricted up-and-down movements.	Neurosis, manic depressive.
Paul came there As did John.	With high and narrow capitals at beginning of words.	Constrained ambition, shyness.
Harry went to See Edith	Left or right slant or change of slant.	A self-struggle is indicated. An attempt to become master of one's moods, drives and ambivalence.

NORMAL WIDTH

A normal width of script is one in which the distance between the downstrokes of a letter is equal to the height.

Positive Example	Description	Indication
please take more of	Normal or moderate width.	Extroversion, uninhibited, healthy self-possession, able to control self consciously without any sacrifice of poise.

IRREGULAR WIDTH *alternative*

Irregularity of width is indicated when the sequence of narrowness and width in the same writing is irregular. It indicates emotionalism.

Fullness and Leanness

Your handwriting may vary from the forms you were taught either in fullness or leanness. A handwriting is considered full when the writing movement encloses a larger surface than that prescribed by the school standard, mainly in looped letters. When the opposite takes place, the handwriting is lean.

Fullness is indicative of fantasy, leanness of reason. Different combinations of fantasy and reason are possible. It is important to observe in which zone the fullness and leanness occur.

FULLNESS

Positive Example	Description	Indication
things of beauty	Full forms.	An imaginative mind, a rich inner life, good memory, inclination to cheerfulness.
when you tell	With pasty pressure.	Sensual, possesses a rich mind and a good imagination.

Example	Description	Indication
of some great	With original letters and disconnected writing.	Original, creative ideas, able to put them to use, intuitive thinking.
the nine of	With simplifications.	Colorful imagination and fine intellect.
Emily	With large size.	Visionary ideas and imagination with ambition to put them to work.
like he too	Fullness in upper zone.	Imagination, vision, colorful speech, cheerfulness, perception, intuition.
small and	Fullness in middle zone.	Warmth of feeling, genial and sociable nature, affection, emotionality, rich emotional life.
your going	Fullness in lower zone.	Sensuous, lively and active imagination.
for easy	Fullness in lower zone, with heavy pressure.	Erotic fantasy, imprudence, strength.

Negative Example	Description	Indication
things of beauty	Full forms.	Indulgence in daydreams, lack of external and self-criticism, lack of clarity in thinking, boastful.
our plans were not	With low form level.	Undisciplined emotions, oversensitive, excitable.
can all her	With illegible writing.	Does not think in a reasonable and clear manner.
Lillian	In upper zone.	Daydreams, exaggerated and inflated imagination, bombast.
small and	In middle zone.	Conventionality, social climbing, amiability.
your going	In lower zone.	Earthiness, sensuality, dreams about money, material and sexual matters.

LEANNESS OR MEAGERNESS

A handwriting shows leanness or meagerness when its forms and movements take up smaller spaces than those prescribed by the school model, as shown in narrow loops, straight lines and angles.

Positive Example	Description	Indication
someday if he	Lean writing forms.	Theoretical thinking, rationality, critical sense, clarity of concepts, intellectual soberness, asceticism.
to be with	In upper zone.	Capacity for abstraction and ideas, rational thinking, critical sense, ethical tendencies.
are all now in	In middle zone.	Emotional control, discrimination, matter-of-factness, weak emotions.
paying for	In lower zone.	Concentration, intensity of attention directed to reality and the essential, sexual sublimation, ethical demands, business-minded.

Negative Example	Description	Indication
someday if he	Leanness of writing forms.	Lack of imagination, dryness, poverty of inner resources, weakness of memory, prosaic minded.
most of the vases	With arcade form.	Lack of objectivity, advantages and disadvantages of one-sidedness.

all the heads of	Leanness of upper zone.	Lack of imagination, lack of form sense, poverty of ideas, dryness, moral or religious seriousness.
over in a new	In middle zone.	Rigidity, coldness; sober realist, often unimaginative and uninspired; matter-of-factness, lack of feeling and generosity, poverty of inner resources, weak emotions.
one in a season	Extreme leanness in the middle zone.	Arid.
of going by plans	Leanness in lower zone (no loops).	Materialism, sexual repression, pessimism, neurotically sharp conscience.
many people of	Unusually lean in the forms of writing.	Sensually cold, stunted instincts; often confused; timidity, discouragement and uncertainty.

Letter Formations

There are four different kinds of letter formations: simplified, enriched or elaborated, flourished or embellished, and neglected. These four ways of writing letter formations are learned at school and are at work in all domains of life, in our habits, gestures and tendencies. They find expression in interior decoration, in architecture, in the dress of the writer, in everything pertaining to style, in the choice of words, gesticulating, and social behavior. They reveal a person's power of judgment, critical evaluation, his degree of maturity and style.

SIMPLIFICATION

When a person modifies the standard letters by eliminating the nonessentials and accessories, reducing them to basic forms without impairing the legibility of the script, simplification is achieved. As there is a desire to cut out the unnecessary parts of the letters and emphasize the essential, it is considered an intellectual achievement.

Positive Example	Description	Indication
Simplify to be here	Simplified.	Purposeful, economical person; matter-of-fact, intelligent, with a mature attitude to life, able to objectively distinguish between what is important, appropriate and pertinent. Sense of order, concerned with the essential.

Negative Example	Description	Indication
Simplify to be here	Simplified.	Lack of form sense, utilitarianism.

ENRICHING (ELABORATION)

The person who enriches his letter forms also stresses the essential and eliminates the superfluous, with this difference: he will use a decorative emphasis which will enhance or adorn the essential without impairing legibility.

We must be careful to distinguish between enriched writing and mere flourishes by deciding whether the additions enhance or detract from the script, and whether they are imaginative additions or superfluous embellishments.

Positive Example	Description	Indication
Water	Enriched.	Cultivated tastes, love of beauty, sense of arrangement, adding what is pleasing and decorative, selectiveness.

Negative Example	Description	Indication
Water	Enriched.	Formality, verbosity, lack of simplicity, lack of objectiveness.

FLOURISHED (EMBELLISHED)

The writer who uses flourishes stresses the unessential parts of letters or craves expression and production of letter forms with embellishments.

Flourishes symbolize the writer's attempt to compensate for an inferiority complex or lack of self-confidence. They are often found in conceited and pretentious people who are impressionable, impressed by affluence and socially prominent people. There is a craving for originality.

Positive Example	Description	Indication
Dear Mark	Flourished.	Craves expression in his own way, and originality; thinks in ornaments.

Negative

Dear Mark   Flourished.

Stresses and emphasizes
the unessential and the
unnecessary, lacks a sense of
proportion; uncultured
tastes, overestimation of
trifles. Predilection
for cheap effects, the showy,
flashy and gaudy;
lacks a clear realistic view
of life, appreciates quantity
more than quality.
Vanity and pretension.

NEGLECTED

When important letter forms are omitted, it is neglected writing.

Negative *Example*	*Description*	*Indication*
	Neglected.	Neglected sense of aesthetic appreciation and appropriateness. Inactiveness, lack of punctuality, disorderliness, unreliability.
	In quick tempo.	Thoughts follow one another with such rapidity that they cannot be written down quickly enough, showing little consideration for the reader. Confusion and indistinctness of ideas, lack of self-assurance and confidence, and an inability to sense importance of detail.
	In slow tempo.	Untidiness, thoughtlessness, carelessness; used by criminals who want to conceal.

The Extrovert and Introvert

The extrovert and introvert are two great divisions of human personality. They differ and are opposite in outlook and approach to life, in emotional needs and expression.

The extrovert has a social nature: his energies are directed outward, he is drawn to his fellowmen, and he goes forward to meet life. He is spontaneous, emotionally responsive, and expansive, subject to influence from his fellow beings, and able to express his feelings freely. His emotions are less complicated than the introvert's and he reveals his reactions quickly. His sex urge is stronger than the introvert's because his emotions are stronger and his nature is directed toward others. The same expression is present in his handwriting. It will lean to the right, and the size will be medium to very large and the rhythm and other graphic features will also describe his nature, as will be illustrated. The more extroverted he is, the more the slant will be rightward.

An introvert is less adaptable to the outer world. Unable to socialize, he gets away from people and retires into himself. Being introspective, he is concerned with his own thoughts. He is more difficult to know than the extrovert because he lives an intense inner life. His energies flow inward; his inhibitions and repressions prevent him from expressing his emotions and inner self. Reserved, highly emotionally sensitive to criticism, he fears being hurt by others, is usually secretive and often selfish, and will cringe before realities.

The same expression is present in his handwriting; it will lean to the left or be vertical, usually small in size, and have other graphic features that will be illustrated. As most introverts are disillusioned and have lost faith in their fellowmen, are skeptical with a negative outlook on life, they usually write with an extremely backhand slant. A highly sensitive introvert will slant his writing

75

predominantly rightward, and the writing will have a narrow, pressed-together aspect. The introversion here will be accentuated by the sensitivity which the far rightward slant reveals.

These are definitions of the 100 percent, or pure, introvert and extrovert, of which there are comparatively few. Most people show a decided tendency or predominance in one or the other direction.

In mature life, the extrovert begins to be a little more introverted and the introvert more extroverted. This is the normal course. In other words, both types tend to reach a compromise in the ambivert, one who displays both introverted and extroverted qualities. In the strict sense of the word, an ambivert combines these qualities in equal proportions, but such a person is exceedingly rare.

For a man to find himself means he has become aware of his relationship and kinship with the world around him and has ceased to think of himself as isolated from others, that is, he has learned to become partially extroverted. The introvert who has not changed after he reaches thirty-five and the extrovert at about thirty are in danger of becoming stunted in their emotional development and are likely to become abnormal.

A really happy marriage is rarely achieved by a predominant extrovert and a predominant introvert, because their basic differences of outlook and approach to life are too difficult to bridge: they will find the gulf too wide between them. The best chance for a lasting and harmonious marriage is between people belonging to the same type of personality, because of similar outlook on the world, similar tastes, needs and interests which form a sound basis for mutual understanding. But first in importance, they must be emotionally and physically well mated.

THE EXTROVERT

As the extrovert chooses a goal that brings him into contact with people, he has an advantage over the introvert in most business positions. He has the self-confidence and the adjustability in contact with others that count for as much as, or more than, knowledge and ability in getting ahead. The extrovert possesses those traits which enable him to make friends easily, and this ability frequently has a relationship to success in business.

Positive Example	Description	Indication
will go to see a spot at	a. A decided right slant, b. wide connections between letters, c. wide letters, d. long ending strokes, e. small even spaces between words, f. medium to large size, g. open ovals, *a* and *o*, h. well-developed lower loops, i. pressure heavy or light, j. legible, superior form level, k. regularity.	Sociable, friendly, in rapport with the exterior world, likes and needs people, warm, desire to give (generosity), self-confidence, prefers activity to contemplation, clear thinker, intelligent, conscientious, aptitude for salesmanship and working in contact with the public.
wells	Very large size, in any slant.	Vitality, physical activity, good share of extroversion.
what	Large size.	Outgoing, animation, courage, initiative, pride, altruism, expansive, imaginative, interested in big matters rather than in detail.

fairly	Vertical large size.	Mostly extroverted qualities which offset the introverted ones.
will go to	Decidedly rightward, same as first example in positive column.	Gregarious, talkative, impulsive, quick in making decisions, tendency to carelessness, could overlook details, impatient.
see a spot		
wells	Very large size.	Excessive pride, likes to be heard and seen; tastes lean to the ceremonial, the grandiose, luxurious and flamboyant; extravagant, restless, wayward. Dancers usually write like this.
what	Large size.	Audacity, nonconformity, self-satisfaction.
fairly	Vertical, large size.	Some interest in people but usually impersonal and detached.

THE INTROVERT

The introvert has in him more originality and depth than the extrovert but needs the quality of extroversion to put his ideas into execution and to make a better adjustment to the conditions of his life.

Vocationally, the introvert can fill a confidential and technical position. He could be a purchasing agent and is best suited to sedentary occupations. Because of a need for self-expression and emotional release, he is often found in creative fields.

Positive Example	Description	Indication
You and Walter may go to the	a. Left slant, b. sizable even spaces between words, c. closed ovals, *a* and *o*, d. short terminals, e. upper right stroke turns inward to the left of capital *W*, f. the *t* bar convex (bowed).	Reflective, analytical, imagination, reason prevails, attention to detail, careful. Vocationally suited to the arts, writing, research, philosophy.
Can we do as well today	Vertical slant, small writing, light pressure.	Reserved, head rules, keeps emotions in check, complete self-control, independence, self-command, self-reliant, lives in the present, can be friendly but is selective in friendships, subjective.
by the way she was there on Tues.	Decidedly rightward slant, narrow compressed letters, closed *a* and *o*, above-average form level.	

Negative Example	Description	Indication
You and Walter	Leftward slant, same as second example in positive column.	Reserved, some inhibition, self-contained, represses some of his emotions.
Can we do as well today	Vertical slant, same as second example in positive column.	Highly critical, cautious, undemonstrative, detached, indifferent and repressed, lacks spontaneity.

by the way she was there on Tues.

Decidedly rightward slant, narrow letters, same as third example in positive column under "Introvert."

Reserve of extreme sensitivity, emotional, self-conscious, does not confide in others nor make friends easily. Keeps to himself, shy, cautious.

Harry did as. he was taught

Extreme left slant (backhand), small size.

Strongly introverted, too repressed and inhibited, early environment developed a measure of isolation, desire for privacy, interested in things rather than people, introspective, reserve borders on self-defense and defiance which may have followed a disillusionment.

THE AMBIVERT

Positive Example

Description

Indication

on the many things she did

Right slant, small size, angular.

Emotionally extroverted, mentally introverted, mixture of both qualities. Keen intelligence, mature personality.

Negative Example	Description	Indication
He was going to hold the	Change of slant.	Markedly changeable in feeling and mood, at times outgoing, other times withdrawn, has not achieved a balance between the contradictory sides of his nature, immature in reactions. Neurotic trends. Has introverted and extroverted tendencies. Indecision and lack of willpower prevent him from developing into a consistent character.

The Capital Letters

Capital letters have more significance when their deviation from the school model is apparent. These letters represent the way you want the world to think of you and what you long to be. The exception is the capital *I* used as the first person pronoun, which expresses how you feel about yourself.

Capital letters must be considered from the point of view of size in relation to the small letters and also of the proportion of the capital *I*. If you write a large capital and a smaller capital *I*, you overcompensate for your feelings of inadequacy by acting self-confident and self-assured. (You put on a "front" to hide your sense of inferiority.) If you write with a large (tall) capital *I* and smaller capitals, you lack self-confidence but have a big ego.

The capitals reflect your mental capacity, good or bad taste, feelings of inferiority or superiority, whether you are talented, original or conventional, old-fashioned or modern in temperament, and your education or lack of it. Capitals can be made simple, printed, ornate (ugly or attractive), plain, original, distorted, very large, large, medium, small, and very small.

Positive Example	Description	Indication
Along	Printed in cursive writing.	Creative ideas.
A	Rounded block letter.	Constructive mind.
A	Simplified, printed.	Culture.
A	Old-fashioned.	Maternal or paternal instincts, found in philanthropists and welfare workers; respect for tradition.
B	Simple, open at bottom.	Generous.
C	Rounded.	Idealism and gracefulness.
<	Angular, top and bottom.	Quick, clever realist.
C	Square.	Interest in building and mechanics.
C D E F J K L P R T V W Y Z	Printed.	Cultured, good taste, constructive talent, mental independence. Intelligent, reader of books; simplicity, exacting nature.
G	Plain and large.	Self-reliant, strong sense of personal pride.
G	Open at the top.	Frank, generous, talkative, may not keep a secret.
E	Greek *E*.	Culture, good taste.
G	Capital *G* in the form of figure eight.	Adaptable, rapid thought, culture.
G	Printed *G*.	Reader of books.
H	Square-shaped *H*.	Logical, practical, independent. Hates frills.

H	*H* with vertical strokes wide apart.	Determined, forceful, courageous.
K	*K* with knot.	Thoroughness.
K	Second stroke shorter.	Ambition.
L	Printed.	Culture, artistic taste.
L	Large upper loop.	Generosity and sensitiveness.
O	Simple.	Balanced and clear thinking.
O	Open.	Frank.
P	Hatlike top on capital *P*.	Idealism, inspiration.
2	*Q* in shape of numeral two.	Mathematical mind, method, precision.
R	Inflated loop.	Protective nature, good family man or home-loving mother.
S	With extra stroke or loop.	Expansive, outgoing nature.
S	Open at bottom.	Expansive.
S	Printed.	Constructive.
S	In form of G clef.	Found in writing of musicians and those liking music.
S	Tall, uniquely constructed.	Imagination and original ideas.
V W	Angular, simplified.	Clear, penetrating brain.
Beam	Capital connected to small letter.	Altruistic.
Beam	Capital disconnected from small letters.	Observant, pause before action.
Robert	Tall, about twice the height of small letters.	Pride, self-respect, dignity, ambition, independence.
Robert	Slightly higher than small letters.	Modesty, simplicity, reserve, poise, adaptability.

Val

| | Terminal that covers the following letter or letters. | Masculine instinct to protect and dominate. Sometimes seen in female writing where circumstances have forced a masculine role. |

Negative Example	*Description*	*Indication*
a A	Open at top.	Talkative, inaccurate.
A	Overlapping strokes.	Inexact, unconventional.
A	Narrow.	Shyness, inhibition.
A	Starting with an arc.	Greed.
B	Upper bulb smaller than lower bulb.	Gullible, often found with open *B*.
B	Upper bulb larger than lower.	Cautious, skeptical, often found with closed *B*, *A* and *O*.
B	Closed at bottom.	Caution.
B R	With long initial stroke.	Less self-assurance than shown to the world. Proud, a prop for writer.
B	Inflated at right side.	Inflated ego.
e	Initial stroke and enrollment.	Calculating mind.
C	With loops at top and bottom.	Mediocre person.
D	Wide open at top without loop.	Talks without thought of consequences.
D	Closed at top with large loop.	Caution, reserved, secretive.
D	With flying loop at top.	Flirtatious, capricious.
E	Severe *E*.	Severity in clothes.
E	Angular *E*.	Rigidity.

	Ornate and ungraceful.	Vulgar taste, ornamental in appearance and surroundings, love of display, mediocre talents, shallow intellect, vanity, poor sense of proportion.
	Arc to the left at the bottom.	Avoids responsibilities.
	Vertical strokes close together.	Fear dominated, won't take chances. Timid.
	Very narrow.	Shyness.
	Involved.	Can get out of tight places.
	Inflated bottom loop.	Vanity.
	Initial stroke touches letter.	Heavy strain in mastering affairs.
	No loop on S.	Mentally lazy.
	Form of dollar sign on S.	Money-minded.
	Left-tending stroke unduly long on capital.	Dishonesty sign.
	Capitals where they ought not to be.	Disorder, exaggeration.
	Very tall, more than three times the height of small letters and/or inflated or flourished.	Pride, vanity, self-esteem, conceit, affectation, pretension, egotism, exaggeration, assertiveness, arrogance; wish to be admired, love of luxury.
	Capital small, not more than twice the size of small letters.	Timid nature, lack of self-esteem.
	Hook on terminal.	Vindictive, mean.

THE CAPITAL I

The capital *I* as a personal pronoun reflects your ego, your self-image, how you think and feel about yourself. It is a complete word in itself and probably the most frequently used one in the language.

Its size, whether small, medium or large, has great significance. It is measured in relation to your small letters and the other capitals in your writing. A simple, moderate-sized *I*, approximately two and a half times the size of the small letters and the same height as the other capital letters, indicates confidence without vanity.

The capital *I* has a multitude of variations and requires special study. Even one specimen of writing can show variations in shape and size. Simplicity in the capital *I* reflects modesty and refinement. Exaggerated loops and artificial flourishes express ostentation. The greater your individuality, the more unique will be the way you form your capital *I*.

The capital *I* can be written small, medium, large, very large, cramped, narrow-looped, inflated, ornate, simplified, printed, angular, round, crossed out, open and closed, tall or short—all revealing the quality of your self-esteem.

Positive Example	Description	Indication
I am	Made simply, in proportion to the small letters.	No pretensions, likes to cooperate with others.
I	Simplified, a single stroke.	Strong ego, plain taste, sophistication, simplicity.
I am glad	Single stroke with good form level.	Very intelligent, direct, straightforward, self-assured, good insight. Sense of essentials.
I should be	Printed, in cursive writing.	Good taste, resourceful, originality of thought and ideas.

But I	Same height and size as other capitals.	Balanced ego, good self-confidence without egotism. Self-respect.

Negative Example	Description	Indication
Q	Full, large, inflated loop in upper zone.	Egotism, exaggerated sense of own importance, usually irritating to others.
But I	Smaller in size than rest of capitals.	Overcompensates for feelings of inferiority or inadequacy by acting self-assured. A withdrawing ego.
But I	Larger than other capitals in size and height.	Lacks self-confidence yet has a big ego.
I	Small, cramped.	Inferiority feelings, weak ego, self-conscious.
i and Thom	Made like a small *i*.	You think of yourself as unimportant. Self-devaluation.
Q	Enclosed like a circle.	Introversion, desire to protect your ego.
I	Closed in upper and lower loops.	Wrapped up in self.

THE CAPITAL M

No single capital letter except the capital *I* carries greater graphic importance than the capital *M*. This is because this letter can be made in many different ways. Even in one specimen of writing, this letter can be made in a variety of styles.

The capital *M* is composed of three downstrokes which frequently vary in their relative height to one another. Each individual height of these downstrokes in comparison with others reveals a specific trait. The first downstroke represents the I, the ego, the second downstroke represents the social status, the third expresses the feelings of the writer to other people, the public.

Positive Example	Description	Indication
m	All three downstrokes relatively even.	Intelligent, poise, high-minded, good taste, well-rounded personality.
TIT TT	Three vertical strokes, one horizontal stroke.	Refined tastes, likes nice things.
Uu	Angular tops, rounded bottoms.	Keen mind, gentle nature, moral resistance to obstacles.
M	Old-fashioned.	Protective.
m	Gracefully curved beginning stroke.	Sense of humor, friendly.
lu	Original or unusual form.	Striving for originality.
m	Made in three strokes.	Honesty, simplicity and freedom from ostentation.
m m M h	In variety of styles.	Versatile, adaptable, many interests.
m	Large loop but no incurve.	Love of responsibility.

Negative Example	Description	Indication
m	Downward middle stroke shorter than the first and third downstroke.	A careless, superficial thinker who does not go into anything thoroughly.
m	Ornate with flourishes.	Conceited, pretentious, used to attracting attention; vulgar tastes.
m	Broadly made.	Immoderate and wasteful.
M	Narrow, pressed together.	Timid, shy, reserved, sensitive, lack of assurance.

martin

Undersized, like small *m*.

Lack of self-assurance and mistrust of abilities.

Large, looped right to left, incurved in initial stroke.

Conceit and pride, high self-esteem, egotism manifested in sensitiveness in regard to social position. In very sloping hand, indicates jealousy.

Curling initial and end strokes.

Avarice.

First downstroke disproportionately high.

Intellectual conceit, arrogance, excessive pride, social ambition.

Changing angle.

Torn character.

Middle hump higher than first and third.

Not too self-assured, relies upon appraisal and appreciation of others.

Third mound or hump rounded and higher than others, if in rounded hand.

Desire for self-assertion and a position of authority, but approach is gentle.

Where last mound or hump is sharp and pointed.

Self-assertive where least expected; will show authority in situations where there is only superficial knowledge. Can become querulous. Seen in neurotic handwriting.

Middle or second mound is lower.

Sets more reliance upon public than on individual opinion.

The second and third mound descend.

Ambition and pride in accomplishment.

Middle downstroke plunging downward, below base line.

Mediocrity, materialism.

Mary

End stroke going back and crossing the letter if in signature.

Suicidal tendencies.

Mary	The first downstroke high, with the bases of the first and second hovering in the air without touching the base line.	Excess of self-confidence and insistence upon being treated respectfully by others, but his good opinion of himself does not in fact stand on solid ground and is forced.
In	First mound higher with narrow incurve.	Family pride, dignity, sensitivity.
m	Made in four parts.	Under mental strain.
m	Small circle at the beginning stroke.	Jealousy, self-centered. (The jealousy is toward one individual.)
m	Large circle in the beginning stroke.	Professional jealousy.
m	Second or third downstroke retraced or covered.	Conceals thoughts.
m	Exaggerated and over-elaborated.	Love of gaudy display, uncultured.
m	With abrupt final.	Energy, combativeness, self-assured, critical.
m	End stroke down to right, below the base line.	Obstinate, short-tempered.
M	Large hooked beginning stroke.	Greed, egotism.

The Small Letters

The letters *a, c, e, m, n, o, r, s, u, v, w,* and *x* belong to the middle zone and do not have an upper or lower extension. The middle zone is the basic zone, as it supports the whole handwriting.

There is no letter that does not constitute part of the middle zone. The small letters often reveal more than other aspects of the writing and indicate your disposition and temperament, whether you are talkative or secretive, honest or deceptive, gullible or cautious, broad-minded or narrow-minded, a deep or shallow thinker.

The small letters can be simple, involved, clear, printed, original, round, narrow, angular, cultured, or ornate, and they also vary in size. Since we cannot discuss each letter of the alphabet in detail, only the most frequently used and significant will be shown.

Positive Example	Description	Indication
a o	Lightly opened at the top.	Frank, talkative, generous when emotions are involved.
a o	Mostly closed.	Not talkative, discreet, diplomatic, can keep a secret.
at a party of one	Sometimes open, sometimes closed.	Sincere person who is neither talkative nor reticent. Can keep a secret.
a o	Broadly made.	Broad viewpoint and thinking. First-rate imagination in a practical science.
c	Round *c*.	Gentleness.
c c	Angular *c*.	Keenness, mental development.
ε	In Greek form.	Refinement, aims for cultural advancement.
Enter	Greek *e* when shown with another form.	Versatility.
l	Closed like an *i*.	Mentally keen, secretive.
m n	Curved beginning stroke.	Sense of humor.
m n	Angular top and bottom.	Sharp mind, analytical ability, concentrated thinker.

	Description	Indication
uu u	Pointed top, round bottom (like *w*).	Good comprehension, executive ability, adaptable to circumstances.
uu u	Long needle points on tops.	Deep, penetrating thinker.
m	Flat tops.	Creative, manual skill.
r	Broad square *r*.	Visual sense, concerned with appearance, creative, talented, often seen in writing of engineers and those with manual skill.
e	Like the letter *e*.	Artistic interest or appreciation.
r, r, R	Broad *r* with other *r*s.	Versatility.
r	Left downstroke higher than right.	Inquiring mind.
r	Quick *r*.	
r	Round on top.	Genial.
r	Sharp top.	Critical mind.
S R A	Printed.	Talented and constructive.
V	Printed *v*.	Cultured mind.

Negative Example	Description	Indication
a a	Very widely open at top.	Too talkative, outspoken, would gossip.
a	Closed with stroke covering top.	Covers up, evasive.
a	Closed at bottom making a complete circle.	Closes up like a clam, keeps a poker face, yet will talk without revealing important secrets.
beautiful	Letter *a* larger than other small letters.	Jealousy.
a a	Open at the bottom (rarely seen).	Dishonest, fraudulent, the embezzler.

	Narrow.	Narrow thinking.
	Involved oval, sliced, two loops; also strokes going into oval.	Dishonest sign, deceptive, misrepresents.
	Double curved oval.	Inhibition and frustration.
	Loop at end of letter *a* and on top of *o*.	Secretive, won't admit anything.
	Loop at beginning of letter. Retraced or repeated at first stroke.	Self-deceit.
	Third stroke higher than first two.	Self-conscious.
	Middle hump higher.	Jealousy.
	Narrow.	Timidity.
	Short points at the top of *m* & *n*.	Not a penetrating thinker; merely covers the surface.
	m too spread out.	Bluffer.
	Very round on top.	Immature, childish, naive, lacks mental acuity, slow thinker, yielding, follows rules.
	Last stroke or hump does not reach base line.	Lacks mental discipline. Cannot consistently bring thoughts down to earth and keep them there.
	Second stroke considerably higher than the first.	Immature, childish.
	Last stroke does not reach base line.	Often conceals facts, afraid to expose thoughts.
	s with very sharp point on top.	Very sharply critical, often mentally cruel.
	s closed with loop.	Caution.
	Open at bottom.	Gullible, has same significance as small open-lipped *b*.

⌣	*v* spread out.	Bizarre imagination, some originality.
moster (for monster)	Omitting letters in words, especially if frequent.	Brain damage.
halth (for health)		
one ± of the many too times tht that he	Many words crossed out or rewritten.	Emotionally disturbed.

THE SMALL LETTER *g*

The letter *g* is unique among the small letters which start in the middle zone and extend into the lower zone. From this letter, the extent of your relationship to love and sex can be determined.

The ideal small letter *g* is made with the following graphic signs:

1. An oval in the middle zone which shows emotional warmth.

2. A strong downstroke which indicates good physical health and self-control.

3. A proper connection of the upstroke with the downstroke in the base line, indicating an ability to abandon oneself to the instinct.

Any departure from any part of a stroke in this letter indicates a departure from the normal pattern of love. There are innumerable variations.

Lower loops may change from one form to another as a result of development changes, psychotherapy or medication. Any number of circumstances may activate inhibiting factors or influence the writer's mood or interest in sexual activity.

Other graphic features such as slant, pressure, etc., can help to illuminate the psychosexual makeup of the writer. Monotonous regularity in the size of the lower loops in a specimen of writing indicates a dull temperament or overcontrol, whereas marked irregularity reveals extreme excitability and lack of control.

Positive Example	Description	Indication
g	Well-proportioned.	Friendly, genial nature, normal expression of love and sex.
g	In the form of a figure eight.	Adaptable, fluency of thought, culture, literary taste.
g	Upstroke to the right.	Altruistic, sympathetic, interest in people, can aid in constructive projects.
g	Upstroke short and to the right.	Initiative, aggressive.
g	Strong downstroke.	Determined.
g	Arc to the right.	Constructive mind, puts visions into effect.
g	Like a figure nine.	Mathematical ability, good judgment.

Negative Example	Description	Indication
g	Too narrow an oval in the middle zone, long lower extension.	Restless, unsatisfied sexual desires, disturbance of the love life.
g	Too small or scanty in lower zone.	Lack of vitality and drive. Little interest in sex.
g	Medium-sized lower loop.	Submissive, compliant.
g	Inflated, called "money bag" in heavy pressure.	Strong sex drive, and sex dreams, active imagination, love of money, avarice, physical vanity, activity.

	With light pressure.	Sensuous to music, color, rhythm.
	Overinflated (very wide and full).	Vivid imagination causes exaggeration, may not lie but will discolor things.
	Large, inflated in vertical slant.	Strong sex desires held in check.
	Another form of inflated loop with a flat bottom.	Wants to put everything on a solid material basis.
	Return stroke does not reach base line.	Emotional and sexual frustration, a disturbance in the sex life, incomplete sex life.
	Failure to close lower loop.	Neurasthenic disposition (in males), sex anxiety and irritability due to sexual weakness.
	Upper stroke does not cross base line but bends off to the right.	Sexual resignation.
	Forms sharp angle without leading back to the base line.	Sexual repression.
	Hooklike curls.	Sexual anxieties.

THE LETTER *t* AND THE *t* BAR

The small letter *t* is the most significant letter of the alphabet. You can get more facts about yourself from this letter than from any other single letter.

The *t* bar is the principal feature. The way it is crossed, its position on the stem, whether ahead of or behind the stem, its length, and the energy spent on making it, determine its value, positive or negative. The way the *t* bar is crossed also applies to the capital *T*. Because the variety of the *t* bars and possible combinations are innumerable, only those generally used will be shown. The *t* bar reveals your willpower and directed energy or lack of it, whether you are a strong or weak person, and whether you are well adjusted or not.

Willpower is a positive force; it is the most vital asset you possess. If you have it, you are self-disciplined, never enslaved by your impulses or appetites; you have resolution and will be able to do what you want to do. If you are a successful person, your handwriting will show the strong willpower, patient persistence, self-confidence and desire to develop your talents which enabled you to reach your goal. Many people, however, substitute stubbornness, a negative aspect, for a positive will. Willpower is not a gift with which you must be born. It can be attained, developed and strengthened as explained in another chapter, "Is Your Willpower Strong or Weak?"

The letter *t* has a stem. You have to start the letter from this stem, but the initial or beginning stroke is not necessary.

Write this sentence: "Those that take trips attempt to interest others." Then write six other lines in sentence form. Look at your *t* bars and see whether you show positive or negative willpower, as indicated in the following positive and negative columns. (The degree of frequency of a particular *t* bar determines your predominant characteristic.)

Positive Example	Description	Indication
t	Evenly spaced on each side of the stem with same pressure as the stem.	Careful, good control and balance; consistent. When it appears consistently in your writing, you give attention to detail.
t	The same crossing but longer on each side of the stem.	A more self-confident attitude, individuality in action, decisive.

t	Long, heavy pressure.	Energy, aggressive, resolution, strong willpower, forceful, enthusiastic, ardor, sustained effort. You can accomplish a great deal and make a good executive.
t	Very long with same pressure as the stem.	An ambitious nature.
f	Tied in a knot, close to the stem.	Persistency. Won't give up and admit defeat.
t	With a hook at either end.	Tenacity, firm purpose, inflexible determination. Ambition.
T	Above the stem, made with strong pressure.	You dream of big things and expect them, plan far ahead, aim high.
t t	Rising upward, also over it.	Hopeful outlook, ambition, aspiration, imagination. In vertical writing, it is social climbing and snobbishness.
t	Arched (convex).	Excellent self-control, self-mastery, muscular control.
t	Arched (convex) above the stem.	Self-control that has been carefully cultivated and developed. Ability to curb bad habits. You want improvement, keep emotions in check and have a lofty imagination.
t t	X-like, printed.	Creative, inventive, independent.

Negative Example	Description	Indication
$-\!l$	Preplaced (left side of stem).	Weak willpower, procrastination, indecisive, starts things but does not finish, cautious, lives in the past, lacks self-confidence, has passive periods, guilt feelings; often shown in handwriting of neurotics.
$l\!-$	Postplaced (right side of the stem).	Hasty, impulsive, impatient, speedy, animated, enthusiastic, nervous energy, anxious to get things done even before you start. In angular writing, it indicates temper.
t	Postplaced close to stem.	Repression which paralyzes the will so that you seem to lack drive, strong guilt feelings.
$\not{t}$	Looped on stem.	Sensitive, talkative, easily hurt or offended; the greater the loop, the greater the sensitiveness. Wants approval.
$\not{t}$	Open stem at bottom.	Sensitive, takes offense quickly.
$\not{X}$	Star-shaped.	Very sensitive, will use sarcasm as a defense mechanism.
$\not{X}$	Star-shaped but weak; does not go through the stem.	Supersensitive, procrastination combined with indecision and repression.
t	Short, light pressure, weak.	Willpower not developed, takes path of least resistance. No ambition or drive.
$\top\!t$	Long, light pressure.	Spontaneous enthusiasm but without force.

$\mathcal{L}$	Short, light pressure, above the stem.	Daydreamer, has big plans and hopes that don't materialize. Impractical.
t	Low on stem.	Selling yourself short, lack of purpose, shortsighted goal, opinion of self not too high.
$\mathcal{A}$	Wigwam shaped, widely spread apart, firm downstroke, pointed at top.	Stubbornness, won't budge even when you know you are wrong.
t	Short *t* bar.	Restraint, repression, timidity.
$\underline{\quad t \quad}$	Excessively long and heavy.	Tends to domineer, irascible, brutal.
t	Short, very heavy.	Blunt, will make people do what you want, could be a bully.
τ	Lancelike, beginning heavy and tapering off in a fine point.	Sharp-tongued, sarcastic, temper flares up and dies down quickly. Mental cruelty.
t	Beginning thin, ending heavy (thick).	A temper that leads to violence.
t	Slanting down.	Bossy type, always giving orders, domineering, aggressive, argumentative, the fighter, rebel.
$\ell \quad \iota$	Slanting down but does not go through the stem.	Neurotic sign. Aggressiveness takes form of arrogant weakness. Petty, critical, fault-finding.
t	Slanting down, clublike. Heavy pressure.	Brutal temper found in coarse nature.
$\mathcal{S} \quad \mathcal{X} \quad \mathcal{D}$	Return stroke leftward through stem without being lifted from paper.	Readily influenced by someone with a stronger will than your own. Introversion, desire for protection.

ℓ	Downstroke of stem covers upstroke.	Ability to conceal thoughts. Conventional.
t	Two bars on stem, one higher and one lower.	Dual personality.
ℓ	No *t* bar (omitted).	Careless, absentminded, impatient, no willpower, hates detail; a lack of concentration and self-confidence. Poor memory.

THE *i* AND *j* DOTS

Just like the *t* bars, the *i* and *j* dots take many forms. Many of the traits indicated in the *t* bars will be borne out in the way you dot your *i*s.

To make a good solid *i* dot requires mental and physical concentration. Therefore, small as the *i* dot may be, the manner of its shape and placement reflects personality like any other aspect of the writing.

When *i* dots appear consistently in the writing, a good memory is indicated.

Positive Example	*Description*	*Indication*
i	Close to stem and directly over it.	Careful attention to detail, punctual, exactitude, precision, order, good memory, concentration, practical. Lacks imagination, cautious.

ı   Close to stem, heavy.   Careful, exact about details, assertive, aggressive, often a lack of imagination. In heavy pressure, aggressiveness takes the form of cruelty.

ı   High, to the right.   Imagination, enthusiastic, inquiring mind, curiosity, progressive ideas, quick thought, impulsive.

ı   Tent-shaped.   Keen mind with critical faculty.

ı ı ı   Semicircle, wavy.   Sense of humor, fun-loving.

ı   In form of arc, open to the right.   Observation.

Negative Example	Description	Indication
ı	Preplaced (to the left).	Caution, procrastination, hesitation, overly careful, slow thinker.
ı	No dot (omitted).	Careless, poor memory, lack of concentration, absent-minded on conscious level. On deeper levels, it is a blind spot in the memory. You block out certain memories of early experiences because of pain.
ı	Heavy, large.	Materialistic and sensuous nature.
ı	Horizontal, dashed.	Energy.
ı	In form of accent.	Criticism.
ı	Faint dot.	Poor vitality, weak willpower.
in it	Dashed, commalike.	Easily irritated, sarcastic, quick temper.

i	Heavy, downward.	Stubborn, fixed opinions.
i *i*	Dashed, high above the stem, at right or left.	Enthusiasm, imagination, dislike of routine and detail.
it is in this time	Variety of *i* dots.	Versatile, lively, imaginative, dislike of routine, perhaps inconsistent.
i	Club-shaped.	Brutal, mean and sensual nature.
dislike	Circle *i* dot.	Wants to be individualistic or different, a way of calling attention to oneself, manual dexterity, interest in arts and crafts, often designers. Dislikes routine and detail. If handwriting shows emotional instability, you are doing work that doesn't suit you.

THE UPPER LOOPS

The upper loops and all top portions of the capitals belong to the upper zone and include the *i* dots and *t* bars. The letters *b, d, f, h, k,* and *l* (also the letter *t* described in another chapter) form part of both the middle and upper zones. The letter *f* is the only letter that has upper and lower zone loops.

When upper and lower loops are made full-bodied and round, the writer expresses himself fully. When upper and lower loops are contracted or curtailed, the writer restricts himself. The upper loops or upper zone reveal your intellectual and spiritual life, your imaginative powers and creative ideas. When they are bizarre and exaggerated, or flourished, we find mental aberrations, an unconscious flight into dreams and illusions.

The upper zone letters can be made tall, very short, wide, compressed, with or without initial strokes, firm, broken and jagged.

Positive Example	Description	Indication
b b	Tightly closed *b*.	Caution, business ability, secretive, tight-lipped.
d	Small or narrow loop on *d*.	Sensitivity.
∂	Greek *d*.	Culture or a desire for it.
d	Greek *d* curved to the right.	Culture and refinement, love of pleasure.
d	Up and down stroke covered on *d*.	Dignity, pride in self.
d	Tall stem on *d*.	Proud.
d	Short stem on *d*.	Independent.
halted	*d* stem low by comparison with other letters.	Shrewdness.
h	Large, wide upper loop.	Open-minded, the philosopher.
h	High upper.	High ideals, if pointed at top; aspiration, imagination.
l	High and wide.	Sensitivity, emotional nature, musical responsiveness, found in writing of singers.
l d	Very high.	Visionary quality.
live	Loop eliminated in letter l.	Original thinker, good judgment, self-confidence.

Negative Example	Description	Indication
b b	Open-lipped *b*.	Gullible, naive.
b	Outward stroke not finished in letter *b*.	Introspective, you tend to go back into yourself and do not have the ability to project your personality or take a courageous stand objectively.

	b sharp at top and bottom.	Analytical, penetrative but resentful.
	Inverted *b*, *d*, *a*.	Inversion in nature, neurotic trends.
	Narrow and squeezed loops.	Emotionally repressed, inhibition, reserve, timidity.
	Up and down stroke retraced on loop.	Narrow-minded.
	Very wide loop on *d* and *t*.	Easily hurt (touchy), supersensitive, susceptible to flattery.
	Greek *d* ending in a lasso formation.	Culture but also a degree of eccentricity and some stubbornness.
	Retraced halfway up on left side of *h*.	Timidity.
	Extra stroke on *h*, *b*, *f*.	Talkative, chatty.
	Broken loop at top.	Heart ailment.
	Broken loop at the right side.	Fear and apprehension of the future.
	Broken loop at the left side.	Fear and apprehension of the past.
	Jagged loops.	Physical illness, heart condition.
	Broken-backed loop.	Distorted thinker, often eccentric, emotional illness.
	Tall, narrow loops.	Restricted philosophy.
	Angular, square.	Obstinate, aggressive, rigidity.
	Upper loops same height as small letters.	No sense of morals, low level of aspiration and values.
	Short and tall narrow loop combination.	Immoral, will rationalize and make excuses but have a tinge of guilt afterward.

high	Short, lean loop.	Little imagination, practical, moderation, low level of aspiration.
halted	Short, very fat loops.	Gullible, immature.
k	High upper loop cramped in letter *k*.	Religious tendencies with element of superstition.
l	Upper loop amended.	Hypochondria.
k	Large loop on right side of *k*.	Rebellious.
walk	Futile flourishes of upper zone.	Unbalanced and delirious fantasies of the insane.
p	Loop at the top of letter *p*.	Argumentative.
f	Unfinished upper loop on *f*.	Lack of persistence.

THE LOWER LOOPS

The loops in the lower zone reveal your material wants, physical vitality, sex drive, amount of energy expended, judgment, mathematical ability, obstinacy, aggressiveness, persistence and imagination.

They symbolize your instincts and are a movement toward the body. Your libido is revealed here; that is, the things, ideas or people that make life meaningful to you, or what interests you most in life.

The lower loops can be wide, short, long, greatly exaggerated, inflated, ineffectual, without return strokes, turn to the right, turn to the left, and have a loop within a loop.

Positive Example	Description	Indication
Ƴ	Loop eliminated in lower extension of *f*.	Good practical judgment, common sense, ability to get to essentials.
f	Printed.	Artistic, aesthetic.
Ƶ	No loop to right.	Desire to get things done quickly; sympathetic, friendly.
Ƶ *Ƴ*	Reverse.	Fluent thinker.
Pg	Long.	Physical activity, material and practical interests, love of pleasure, sensuousness, ambition, love of variety, restless.
ƴ	Medium long.	Compliant, submissive.
ρ	Long extension, no loop, medium heavy pressure.	Maximum of physical activity and vitality, love of sports.
Ƴ Ƴ	No loop, like numerals seven and nine.	Mathematical ability.
ƴ	No loop, downstroke medium heavy.	Determination, decisive, firm, energetic, speedy, concentration, good judgment, also inhibition and repression of instincts.
ƴ	Right turned.	Altruistic, sympathetic, interest in people, understanding, desire to contribute something to the world.
Ƴ	Short, right turned.	Initiative and aggression.
ƴ	Slender loop.	Selective in friendships, usually those with similar interests.

	Inflated.	Imagination is individualistic, original and results in creativeness, resourcefulness encouraging mental activity, sense of responsibility, obligation and necessity, warmth, realism, technical and practical inclinations.
	Long, slender, graceful.	Line value sense and appreciation.
	Rounded at bottom.	Friendly, gentle, gracious, often naive.

Negative Example	*Description*	*Indication*
	Triangular *f* with horizontal stroke.	Tension, strong reaction against interference.
	Triangular *f* with backhand slant.	Emotionally inhibited, does not experience physical gratification.
	Triangular.	Affectation, snobbish, vanity, fondness of social formality, display of ceremony.
	Reverse figure eight in lower loop of *f*.	Withdrawal, restriction of friendship, thwarting of instinctual drives or material desires, growing determination, quick thought, a homosexual sign.
	With loop at the left side.	Persistent, secretive, critical.
	Inflated.	Fond of pleasure, carefree, lacking in deep feeling.
	Compressed.	Tension and contraction of the muscles, associated with apprehension and strain.

	Broken.	Secret apprehension about sexual and social concepts, conduct and eventualities.
	Short, with light pressure.	Physical weakness, little interest in sex and material matters.
	Short, with heavy pressure.	Lack of drive, passive, matter-of-fact.
	Loop to the left.	Clannish, immature, dependent.
	Horizontal.	Emotionally childish and immature.
	Small loop at end of downstroke.	Clannish, a loner, sexually frustrated, deviation.
	Extremely slender.	Restricted imagination, factual, has difficulty in visualizing.
	Triangular.	Persistent, active, impatient, obstinate, aggressive.
	Loop within a loop.	Persistence which amounts to compulsiveness, continues doing something even after the necessity is no longer apparent.
	y twisted.	Abnormal sex interests.
	Incurve in stem.	Sensitivity, eccentricity.
	Inflated, with light or medium pressure.	Sensitivity to music, color, rhythm; found in graceful dancers. Tendency to make generous gestures.
	Inflated in heavy pressure.	Strong sex impulses, physical appetites.
	Exaggerated.	Exaggeration, vivid imagination magnified out of proportion to true facts; given to theatrics, superficial.

	Reversed.	Impulse to give but caution overtakes writer and he closes the giving channel.
	Extremely long.	Disorganized, unstable, confused.
	Very heavy, thick downstroke at end of stem.	Bluffer.
	Loop does not reach base line.	Sex frustration.
	Upward loop runs close to downward stroke without crossing the base line.	Sex anxiety and irritability caused by sexual weakness.
	Sharp angle at bottom of downstroke without reaching the base line, left slant.	Sex repression.

The Numerals

Written numbers are symbolic of material values. They indicate your attitude toward material values and whether you are a good or poor reckoner or have a talent for monetary matters. Sometimes numerals are more revealing than words.

Positive Example	Description	Indication
7805	Smooth, clear and nimbly written, quick tempo and legible.	A reliable and quick reckoner, mathematical aptitude, talent for monetary matters. Attitude toward material values is reasonable.
32 045	Clumsily and awkwardly drawn in an otherwise fluent writing.	While you are intelligent, you cannot calculate or tackle numbers; likely to make mistakes in the most simple problem, a poor reckoner, no concept of numbers.
Jan. 30	Extremely full numbers, skillfully and nimbly made with libidinous pressure. They are extremely large with inflated loops. The numerals are usually larger than the script.	An extremely strong libido, powerful wish fantasy, insatiable greed, an excessive spender and will not stop at criminal acts in order to satisfy his sensuous aspirations.
3 2	Numbers with embellishments such as extra hooks and curls.	Wastefulness will be accentuated.
3 9 1	Illegibly made.	Disregard for accuracy in money matters. No love for thrift.

Negative Example		Description	Indication
1	1 or 2 ?	Voluntarily indistinct so that they can be mistaken for another figure.	A sign of dishonesty, trickery and cheating.
3	3 or 5 ?		
4	4 or 6 ?		
8	0 or 8 ?		
9	9 or 2 ?		
3 days ago		Mending of numbers in fluent writing.	Dishonesty.

2/15/70	Numbers nimbly made in date and address, etc., but clumsily made when numbers refer to money.	Nervous reaction to financial matters but not dishonest.
$ 38.65		
4 58 Shore St.	Conversely, money numbers more nimbly made than others.	Considerable importance accorded to money; the cult of the dollar.
$ 34.50		

The Beginning Strokes

Beginning strokes of words are also called initial strokes. They symbolize the past. ·

When we first learn how to write cursively (connected) we are taught to use beginning strokes, but as we grow up we discard them. This kind of simplification, i.e., the elimination of the unessential or superfluous, is one of the first steps we take in developing our mental processes and advancing toward maturity. When you see a growing child eliminate the beginning strokes, you may be sure his intelligence is above average.

As you mature, the beginning strokes will be dropped or shortened for practical reasons, revealing that you have become independent. Those who retain initial or beginning strokes in their adult life never grow up (mature) or have a full and successful life. When initial strokes appear in some words and are omitted in others, diversified characteristics are expressed. You may be independent in certain ways and not in others.

Beginning strokes can be short, long, very long, garland, rigid, wavy, hooked, or in the form of a circle.

Positive Example	Description	Indication
m n	Wavy.	Sense of humor, likes fun.
b, h, k, t, v, w, *n, m f. i*	No beginning stroke (omitted in all letters).	Direct, organized, purposeful, uncomplicated; efficient, clear, objective, quick thinking leads to practical, unswerving, simple action. The ability to begin without preliminaries.

Negative Example	Description	Indication
the one who is	Copybook or conventional beginning strokes.	Adherence to conventional concepts, habits, and beliefs. Immaturity. Tension and retention of past experiences, attachment to tradition and dependence upon home environment. Concerned more with detail than with important matters. Wasting time on nonessentials.
right or wrong	Stiff, inflexible, beginning below the base line.	Resentment, the "chip on the shoulder attitude." You are on the defensive trying to shield yourself. Feel imposed upon, impatient and get into quarrels.
here cand cnow	In the form of a large hook.	Acquisitive, built-in antagonisms, indicating that the individual wants recognition.
be here	Ascending left to right.	Contrary, systematic opposition.
one way	Garland form.	Desire to please.

꒐ ꒐ ꒐ ꒐	In form of small circle.	Jealousy focused on one person. When circle is large, jealousy is focused on many.
꒐ ꒐	In form of small hook.	Selfish, egotist, possessive.
꒐ ꒐	In the form of backstroke without loop.	Very sensitive about others hurting you.
꒐ ꒐ ꒐	Short ticklike strokes.	Temper.
Carl	Long beginning stroke to capitals.	Less self-assurance than shown to the world. Proud.

The Ending Strokes

Ending strokes are also called terminals and finals. These strokes end the words and symbolize your social and interpersonal approach, which like the endings themselves, take on many variations, far more than the beginning strokes. Ending strokes usually confirm other findings about the writer.

Ending strokes can be short, long, very long, ascending, rightward, leftward, downward, blunt, hooked, horizontal, heavy, thin, or weak.

Positive Example	Description	Indication
are you	Ascending terminals, long.	Generosity, considerateness, kindness, spirituality, lofty ideals and aspirations, sympathetic.

Example	Description	Indication
uay	Long final on *y* and *g* rising above middle zone in combination with *u* shape of *n* and *m*.	Beneficence.
auy tag	Upward to the right.	Altruism, understanding.
y y t	Forward to the right.	Initiative, speedy action.
hand as	Ending in a sharp rightward movement in the upper zone.	Emancipation, break with the past, started a new way of living.
ate	Brought firmly to base line.	Positive.
The wood or	Beginning and ending strokes omitted.	Practical, wastes no time or effort on unimportant preliminaries.
are you	Variation of the upcurve.	Artistic, probably good in drawing.
is the	Ascending high.	Vivid imagination, spiritual interest, mysticism.
man		

Negative Example	Description	Indication
one final	Too long an ending stroke.	Extreme charity, purely a superficial emotion which goes with a guilt complex.
am at	Ending stroke exaggerated.	Generosity mixed with intolerance.
take	Straight out.	Cautious, refuses to come into too close contact.
a tall	Thick, heavy, long horizontal.	Bitter, resentful, suspicious, bad temper.
he is	Accentuated horizontal, medium pressure.	Can't stop or let go of opinions, habits and worries.
for us	Ascending, very high.	Show-off, exhibitionist, false sophistication.

pass on	Ascending, club-shaped.	Brutality, pugnacity.
th or	Straight up, inflexible.	Suspicion.
d r r	Angular.	Stiffness, jaggedness, smartness.
a man for	Very short or omitted.	Acquisitive, secretive, selfish, inconsiderate.
all the	Short, hooked.	Selfish, tenacious, inconsiderate.
she had	Curled under and hooked.	Interest in self; selfish.
B	Leftward, cat's-paw stroke.	Falseness.
see in that	Blunt and heavy.	Blunt, obstinate, set and unyielding.
my gp	Clawlike stroke.	Avarice.
am sure	Heavy, downward, pointed.	Sarcasm, sadism, destructiveness, violence, revengefulness.
log	Leftward (on top).	Introversion, self-blame.
be far from	Different kinds of ending strokes.	Conflict; something is troubling the writer.
a well		
one for you and	Terminal strokes to fill otherwise blank spaces.	Suspicion.
we hid it	Weak, does not reach base line.	Indecision.
man	Narrow writing with ostentatious final.	Pretended generosity; actually stinginess is indicated.
he had	Long, pointed downward.	Bad temper, sharp tongue, hard to get along with.
some at	Looped final.	Eccentricity; evasive.
at nooy	Flung down.	Brutality, anger, potential destructiveness.

all, the
and it

ated

one and

Whiplash.	Sadism.
Blunt.	Blunt, cruel, bad temper.
Vertical.	Daydreamer, visionary.
With outbursts of pressure.	Aggressive; emotion unbearable. Tensions can be released through criminal acts.

The Signature

Your signature has a place of its own. It is the essence of personality and the symbol of the self. It reveals your aspirations and tastes, how you feel about yourself, how you want to be or appear, how you are, your relationship between yourself as a whole and your social self and even without awareness on your part, it reveals the hidden aspects of your ego. All these are indicated by the relation between your signature and the body of the writing in form, movement and arrangement, in the proportional relation of the given name and the family name and the placement of the signature on the writing paper.

Signatures frequently contain unconscious and unintentional representations of images and symbols which escape your attention. Often graphic symbols of a person's profession are found in the writing of signatures especially when it is the writer's clear-cut dominating idea.

For example, theologians will reveal the sign of the cross: painters, the palette:

Your signature changes throughout the course of your life and it is your legal identification all over the world.

A signature by itself without the body of the writing cannot reveal your character because the writing of the signature may differ from the body of the writing. Therefore it is important to compare both the signature and the writing. Generally traits revealed in your writing will be shown in your signature and more.

Those who write contracts, checks, notes and other documents which obligate them may deliberately deform their signature to make it difficult for forgers to imitate. People who must sign their name frequently may abridge and replace it with a scrawl or stroke after the signature.

A signature usually consists of the given name, the middle name and the family name and many times an appendage, underscore, dot, dash, or embellishment.

Positive Example	Description	Indication
I'll see you on Tuesday. Alice	Signature same size as body of writing without any appendages.	No pretense or veneer, natural, the same in public as in private, the personality and character are the same, sincerity, honesty, reliability, clear thinking.
Frank Winn	Signature legible, plain and clear.	A desire to be understood; modest, sincere, reliable, co-operative, has nothing to hide.
Daniel Morton	Ascending.	Wants to get ahead and to succeed, professionally ambitious.
Martin Brown	First and last name connected.	Makes full use of his whole personality, makes an effective manager or executive, knows how to organize for efficiency.
John Simms	Threadlike connections in signature.	Capable of keen psychological insight, one who instinctively seems to know another's thoughts, can solve perplexing predicaments.
Arthur Bowers	Right slanted.	Individual looks upon sex as natural expression of normal physical feelings.

	Description	Indication
[signature: S Brink]	Original.	Basically artists make practical use of their creative talents.
[signature: Ben Simmons]	Straightline.	Simplicity.

Negative Example	Description	Indication
[handwriting: The package came today; Regina]	Entirely different from the body of the writing (text).	A double nature, desire to conceal one's inner nature with a mask or disguise, shrewd and cunning (there may be a mental disorder.)
[signature: K. L. Brown]	Carefully written or strikingly legible.	Pedantry.
[handwriting: Mary will be here tonight Jack]	Larger in size than the text.	Wants to be recognized as an important figure, indicates pride. When signature is over-large, false pride and pretentiousness.
[handwriting: Mary will be here. Jack]	Smaller in size than text.	More modest than he appears.
[signature: Fanny White]	Flourished or ornamented.	Egotism, vanity, affectation, ostentation, love of display, likes to be in the limelight, secretive.
[signature: D Morrison]	Letters in signature smaller toward the end.	Diplomatic, shrewd.
[signature: H. Slater]	Last stroke goes through signature.	Wants to cancel himself out, hostile toward self, suicidal tendencies.
[handwriting: As far as he could go. J. L. Smith]	Signature left slanted or vertical, script right slanted.	Appears cold and unfriendly but is the reverse (kind and responsive). Attempts to repress responsiveness and suppress the emotions.

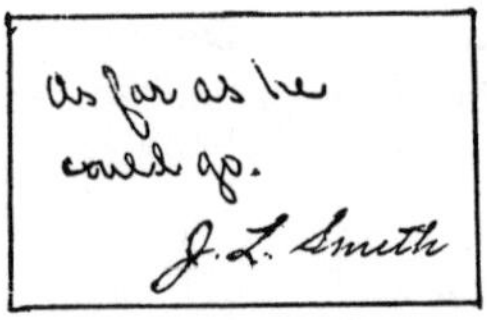 *As far as he could go. J. L. Smith*	Signature right slanted, script left slanted or vertical.	Outwardly friendly and responsive but inwardly reserved. Other features of the script may show that writer is reserved and external behavior is a cultivated act.
 *Martha L. Fisher*	Varying slant in signature, different size of small letters and pressure.	Difficulty in sticking to decisions. Confused about sex, will act differently on different occasions.
 *Ella — Leonard*	With final letters abnormally long or extended.	Overcaution and mistrustful of others.
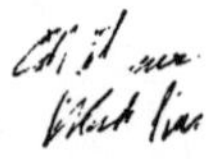 *[illegible signature]*	Signature illegible, especially if script is also illegible.	Evasive, cunning, doesn't want the world to know him, secretive misrepresents, eccentric.
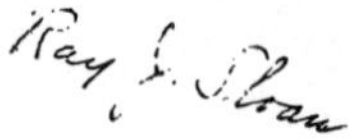 *Ray S. Sloan*	Signature descending.	Fatigue and discouragement, depression may be due to physical illness.
 *Jo ann Sills*	Ascending steps.	Constant struggle against depression.
 *Will N. Orr*	Muddy and heavy strokes crudely formed, capitals, inconsistent pattern.	Abnormality, perversion and sadism.
 *Trace Sands*	Super embellishments.	Neurotic tendencies.
 *Al Finn*	Crossed strokes in signature.	Competitiveness.
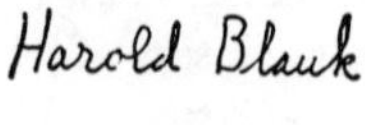 *Harold Blauk*	Vertical slant.	Inhibition about free sex expression since he thinks before he acts.
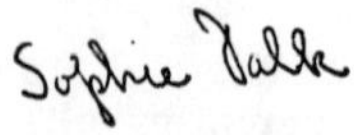 *Sophie Valle*	Left slant.	Negative reaction to sex thoughts.
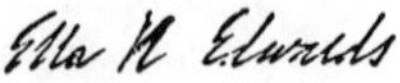 *Ella N. Edwards*	Squeezed letter forms.	Wants his own way in sexual matters and cannot be easily sidetracked.

 Flourished signature.   Likes much
attention.

RELATION OF GIVEN NAME TO FAMILY NAME

The family name represents the social ego, the given name, the intimate part of the ego.

Positive Example	Description	Indication
David John Marks	Good balance between given and family name.	An amicable, reciprocal relation between writer and his environment.
John L Elder	Middle initial included in signature.	Proper sense of dignity.
George Holmes	Capital of given name larger than family name.	Sensitive about his youth.
Robert Paul	First name larger and more embellished than family name.	Narcissistic urge to attract attention.
Sam M King	Undersized capitals of signature.	Lacks self-confidence, doubts abilities, self-devaluation.
Dora Long	First or given name larger than family name in a married woman's signature.	Preference for the unmarried state (or life).

Negative Example	Description	Indication
Max Bell	Family name larger than given name.	Family pride, feelings of prestige, preoccupied with social status.

Arnold J. Strong

Different slant
in first and last
name, also applies
to different widths
in family name
and given name
or any writing
errors that repeatedly
occur in a given name.

Strife within the family.
Conflict between
social and
private life.

The Writing on the Envelope

The writing on an envelope which contains capitals and numerals reveals several important traits of character. It expresses the writer's attitude toward social and public life.

As the writing on an envelope is governed by the purpose that the letter be delivered to the addressee, most people make a special effort to write the address clearly and carefully, especially numerals. However, there are many who write the address so indistinctly that it is almost indecipherable. Such carelessness indicates some psychological difficulties.

A positive indication can only be obtained when the writing and the numerals on the envelope can be read without difficulty.

Positive Example	Description	Indication
Mr. L.P. Brown *356 Elm Ave* *Avon, Ohio 21450*	The address on the envelope has the same size, form and margin as the letter itself.	Writer has a sense of proportion, good taste, culture, breeding, artistic sense, and is the same in public as in private.

Aug 7, 1970
Dear Low :-
        Best
wishes on your
birthday
                Ann

	Legible, clearly written.	A natural, genuine, adaptable, cooperative nature, unconstrained in daily life and in social relations; practical sense, order, method, thoroughness and accuracy.

Mr. D. F. Brown
973 Alton Ave
Stowe, Mass.
10768

Negative Example	Description	Indication

	Illegible and ambiguously written.	Antisocial tendencies. Psychological difficulties in observing conventional considerations, a special difficulty or disturbance in regard to adaptation, characteristic of people who are difficult and troublesome in personal as well as social intercourse; either tactless, obtrusive or clumsy.

	Writing on the envelope larger than writing of letter.	Self-assured or overbearing attitude is a pose that lacks sincerity.

Mr. J. Brown
10 Elm Street
Avon, Ohio

Dear Jay:-
    Send the
dresses to Alice
on Monday
      Joe

Mr T. Brown
10 Elm Street
Avon, Ohio ±1470

Dear Jay:-
    Will
see you
Monday
       Joe

Writing in the letter is larger and wider than on the envelope.

Self-confidence is greater than appears from outward behavior, which is more self-conscious, uncertain and inhibited. May be self-assured in work but in social life has difficulty in asserting himself.

Self-correction

Through Handwriting

Man Changes His World
as He Changes Himself

This then is the end for which I strive to attain to such a character myself and to endeavor that others should attain to it with me. In other words, it is part of my happiness to lend a helping hand, that many others may understand even as I do.

—Benedict Spinoza

We are in a period of tremendous change. This is obvious on a technical level but we are now beginning an era in which social change must keep pace with technical change. The social pattern or set values we inherited from the ancient world do not give happiness in our world today. The turmoil, insecurity, conflict and confusion we now experience are increasing. Thousands of people are breaking down because they cannot cope with the pace and pressures of daily living. Stress and frustration are the by-products of the instability of modern life and ceaseless agitation, leading to mental and physical illness.

Man knows little of the deeper values in his own nature. He is seen as a bundle of complexities. The mind of the average man is far from being an instrument within his control. It is being impressed at all times, even during sleep to some extent, with a picture of a thousand objects claiming his attention. The medical profession agrees that human beings are a prey to acts of auto-intoxication; that is to say, they flood their own systems with various poisons bred by various negative states of mind and emotion and improper ways of living. The most poisonous are the conscious and unconscious states of anger, hate, fear, worry, guilt, envy, greed and insecurity that prevent the deepest levels of human warmth from being approached. From a scientific point of view, these are the breeding places for all instincts that make for war, cruelty, lust and stupidity. The only protection is to develop a higher and stronger vibration of thought and feeling, i.e., to be a positive thinker and willer and a master of ourselves.

The emotions of man are far more powerful than the mind. The emotions have never been educated. We have marvelous universities for the training of the mind where individuals are taught skills in the arts and sciences, but the emotions are almost completely undisciplined and immature.

On the physical side, our improper ways of living and eating, the lack of knowledge of what constitutes a good diet, the pollution of air, water and soil, tobacco, alcohol and lack of exercise affect the central nervous system and contribute to widespread disease. There is a law that can be applied to the general problems of disease and human suffering. It is found that behind every disease there is both a defect of character and an error in conduct, which of course means that there is a lack of harmony with the steady movement of the universe when people consciously or unconsciously move against this rhythm. This is one of the deep roots that cause mental or physical imbalance in the personality. From this law, a true means of prevention emerges. If wrong or unrhythmic action, thought and emotion produce pain and illness, then right thought, emotion and action produce happiness and health. Prevention is obtained by continued right conduct and action, which means wise and, above all, kind conduct.

Hence, real cure consists in correcting the error in conscious-ness, the defect in character, and ultimately eliminating from one's life pain-producing action, especially emotional stresses, misuse of the body, and cruelty. Therefore we must first learn how to take care of the body and keep it well, not to overwork it, nourish it properly with good food, and always keep it clean. Without a healthy body, you cannot work hard or bear the strains and pressures of daily living. However, it must be you who control the body and not the body that controls you.

In mastering ourselves, we must put the mind in order and train it to work clearly and dispassionately and establish a true perspective on life. We must clear out of our minds all the accumulated rubbish so that we can have a clear field in which to develop our latent powers. We must get rid of our inhibitions and all our false values, uncertainties, indecisions and restlessness, and all those states which eat away the vitality of the body and mind.

Many of us have turned to psychologists and psychiatrists to analyze the root of our troubles. All of these men do all they can for us because we have given them to believe that we do not care to learn the truth, namely that we could do much more for ourselves than they can do. Within each individual is the eternal self with powers yet to be developed; but man has not yet realized his strength or greatness, nor does he see except dimly the heights to which civilization can reach.

A desperate need exists today for an understanding of man's essential nature. Self-analysis and proper understanding of the workings of the mind and body are needed for the attainment of the ethical values of life. Above all, man must know himself, his faults, his weaknesses and his pathway in life; and he must have an adequate self-image to enable him to depend on himself, his own efforts, powers and resources, if he is to realize his creative potentialities. Creative ideas lie within man's self and any inhibition or resistance to self-knowledge prevents free access to the fertile source of his abilities, which impoverishes and deprives him of opportunities for self-realization and peace within, and results in self-defeat.

While introspection is necessary for self-understanding, one should be neither morbid nor excessively interested in his mental and emotional states. Yet it is a hopeful sign that men who have subjected themselves to humiliating and honest introspection have emerged as improved personalities.

All of us are conditioned in one way or another. Living is actually a dynamic cycle of condition, decondition and recondition. In other words, this means learning, unlearning and relearning. Unlearning is one phase of keeping up a healthy state of mind, but we still have to reeducate ourselves. Only the man who can continually adjust his mind and emotions to the shifting needs of the times can cope with the complexities of modern life and avoid neurosis.

We must learn that man changes the world when he changes himself. Biology shows that all living organisms, no less than the universe itself, are subject to the laws of change. While it is very difficult to change oneself and overcome bad habits, and not everyone will do it, there are many who can and will do some deep thinking on their own and exert tremendous energy to bring about a psychological change in themselves. One outstanding example of an individual who changed himself and also helped others to change, inspiring many powerful minds, is Benedict Spinoza, the seventeenth-century Dutch philosopher who gave the world one of its greatest philosophies.

Our personalities are made of our habits. In a sense we are our habits and our habits are largely ourselves, but they do not have to remain static. We can change our habits when we change ourselves. "We literally become new creatures and one of modern psychology's more encouraging discoveries is that we can form new habits at any time of life. This means that at any time of life we can make decisive changes and improvements in our personalities," says Geoffrey Hodson in *The School of Wisdom*. "When man successfully probes his own nature back to the Center and Core, he finds a single source of all men, all beings, all existence. Unity emerges as the supreme truth. All are part of one stupendous whole."

In our present age we cannot perceive this spiritual fact. So man fights and destroys. He is at war with himself and the world. The League of Nations failed to prevent war, and peace is as yet not natural with all men. But despite its denial by men, the fact of "oneness" remains, and from that unity and source man's divine nature can unfold. There would be no racial discrimination and no divisions in religion if man realized this fact of unity. Relations between individuals would change, leading to a more peaceful and happy life.

To be a mature adult is to join the brotherhood of man.

This binds one mentally and spiritually with his fellowmen and with nature and at the same time endows him with powers which he can use for character correction.

Character correction and character building largely consist of redirecting the energy from its destructive, discordant, harmful and negative expression, to its constructive, harmonious and positive manifestations. Positive and negative thinking are merely two ways of using the same mind through the power of self-choice. Positive thinking is direct, affirmative, sure of itself and moves straight toward its objective.

While there has been much self-improvement literature in recent years, most of it has been of little value to the people who need it most. The reason for this is that there are no universal formulas for self-help. Each person is a unique individual who operates in his emotions, responses, habits, thoughts, and motivations and actions differently from others. When a person comprehends the workings of his own emotional, mental and physical forces and sees himself as he really is, he has a chance of expanding his consciousness, leading to keener intellect, positive emotions, and faith in himself which enables him to live a useful and purposeful life. To do anything worthwhile, man must be something, and this is predicated on greater self-knowledge. At such times, all hints of self-improvement work.

Handwriting analysis is one means of isolating and evaluating your character and personality traits, picking out the fears and defenses, explaining your emotional, mental and physical makeup and thus enabling you to see yourself as you are.

Part One of this book has given you sufficient information on handwriting analysis to recognize in your own handwriting the graphic indications or signs which reflect both your strengths and your weaknesses. This knowledge will start you on the road to effective self-analysis.

Part Two describes many of the positive and negative attitudes and how they affect us, and explains graphotherapy, i.e., self-correction through handwriting analysis. You will learn how you can restyle your personality by discarding from your handwriting the negative graphic indications revealed and replacing them with positive ones. In other words, you will see how your faults or bad habits can be overcome by positive thinking directed through the writing exercises outlined in this section.

This redirection of energy is in line with modern ideas on healing and rehabilitation. Psychologists recognize that the technique of writing is therapeutically effective in giving release to the emotions, as a means of self-expression and as a technique for training concentration and attentiveness. People express different aspects of their personality in writing from those they express verbally. Read *Psychosynthesis* by Dr. Roberto Assagioli.

SUGGESTIONS FOR WRITING EXERCISES AND TO HELP YOU EXAMINE YOURSELF

Write down honest replies to the following questions:

1. What are your ideals? In what do you believe?

2. What is your ambition in life and why?

3. Are you prepared to face the truth about yourself and make a change, or are you going to sit on the fence?

4. What are your faults? What are your talents? What are you doing about them?

5. What are the things that affect and worry you? Just how important are they?

6. What steps do you think might solve your various problems?

This self-examination should be preserved until you have all the answers clearly written down. You will find that you have never done so much sound thinking before. The result will be like a tonic to the brain and a stimulant to your endeavors.

The important thing is to clear everything out of your mind which you can possibly do without, in order to concentrate all your powers upon what is strictly necessary.

How to Change Your Personality Through Handwriting

Educate your subconscious mind for it is this alone which directs your life, moulds your character and creates your destiny.
—Dr. Victor Panchet

If you have studied Part One of this book, you have recognized in your own handwriting your abilities, potentialities, type of personality, introverted or extroverted, your manner of working, and your weaknesses and strengths.

You have also come to realize that your difficulties are due to negative attitudes, habits and responses you acquired through the years, many of them going back to childhood. Once you have become aware of these facts, you have taken the first step toward making yourself more nearly what you would like to be.

Since negative habits and thoughts are linked with failure, you now feel a need to destroy them and move in a new direction by laying a more enduring foundation to build on in order to solve your problems and realize your goals.

When we write we do not stop to think of how we write. We are only concerned with the message we wish to convey; but we register positive and negative signs automatically which symbolize our negative and positive thoughts and habits and thus leave a permanent mark on the paper of what the subconscious knows, revealed by the various formations of the strokes in the writing. This is the reason a person cannot cover up the things which lie deep in his character. In spite of repression, the subconscious mind reveals itself sooner or later.

It is important for you to know at the outset that your personality is the sum total of your habits and attitudes and as such can be changed, but you cannot change your basic self, i.e., the individuality or the inner person. Basic character traits in handwriting are indicated in the form of connections, i.e., garlands, angles, threads and arcades, and should be maintained in the handwriting. Extreme changes of slant, i.e., from extreme left to extreme right and vice versa, should be avoided.

If you have observed your writing throughout your life, you will have noted that your handwriting constantly changed as you passed through the various developmental stages and you acquired various traits and characteristics that are now shown in your handwriting. Because traits and characteristics make us write with certain types of strokes, you can force a change of your handwriting by physical change in the formation of the strokes, thereby forcing a change of your personality. Handwriting is also a self-suggesting procedure. By consciously trying to write in a way that expresses the mental and emotional states you want to acquire, you change your personality.

Therefore, if your handwriting reveals any negative graphic sign or undesirable quality, omit or abandon it from your handwriting and replace it with a positive and beneficial one suited to your personality. By consciously writing with positive graphic signs and forming a clear mental image of the desired results with awareness of your goal, you will be observing yourself as you observe your writing, and thereby overcome the negative features.

It has been found by experience that making an effort to refrain from a bad habit or thought reinforces it and that no two thoughts can actively occupy the mind at the same time. Therefore, in order to eliminate a bad habit or thought, you have to put a positive one in its place. As the negative habit or thought disappears, your mind will attract positive thoughts.

The following are specific directions to follow:

1. a. Acquire a relaxed attitude and avoid distractions.

   b. Reflect or meditate a few minutes before you begin to write. It will help you to stir up positive and powerful emotions and will lead you to make resolutions along the lines you wish to follow.

   c. Enumerate your reflections in one or two pages of writing.

2. a. Study your writing and note the various negative graphic signs. Select one of them which you consider most important to overcome and concentrate on it.

   b. Compare the negative sign in your handwriting with the one illustrated in the book for similarity.

   c. Look at the positive column for a positive indication suitable to you and incorporate it in your handwriting, eliminating the negative graphic sign. For example: If you have noted in your handwriting that your base line is wavering and you are aware of the unsteadiness of your emotions and lack of control over them which such a base line indicates and you want to overcome it,

      1. Start to write in a straight base line using lined paper which helps you keep to the line, for ten days.
      2. Then write on unlined paper. Test your writing by turning the paper upside down.
      3. If you are writing in a straight base line, discontinue writing on lined paper.
      4. If your base line is still wavering, continue writing on lined paper for a few days and then test yourself again, writing on unlined paper. Repeat unless you can write in a straight line on unlined paper.

   d. Each trait or sign has a direct bearing on others, for when one is changed the others will also change. When you are able to write in a straight base line which indicates good balance, perseverance, equanimity, self-control and conscientiousness (reliability), you will notice that your small letters become relatively even in size and height, which has a similar indication, and your slant will go in one direction, corroborating these indications.

3. a. Write for one half hour in the morning, if possible, but at least one half hour before retiring at night. This is the best time for the subconscious mind to accept suggestions.

b. After writing your reflections, enumerate in writing what your problems are and what you want to accomplish or overcome for about fifteen minutes and then use the writing exercise or slogan appropriate to your case.

c. Be sure you are eliminating the negative sign and substituting a positive one in your writing. Do likewise for any other writing you may do during the day. The more you write with the positive sign, the more quickly you will acquire it.

d. Elimination is not only the removing of waste products from the body but also the removing of negative emotions, thoughts and attitudes stored in the subconscious. It purifies the subconscious mind. People who hold on tightly to thoughts, feelings and experiences which are no longer for their highest good suffer from stomach and intestinal ailments. Just as the body must let go of whatever it no longer needs, so must the mind. A change of attitude from positive to negative effects a corresponding change in the body. The function of the power of elimination is twofold —to eliminate error in your life and to expand your goals. "Elimination of something from your life is always an indication that something better is on the way."—Catherine Ponder, in *The Healing Secret of the Ages*.

4. IMPORTANT. Eliminate only one negative sign from your writing at one time. Trying to correct more than one trait at a time will definitely cause nervousness and confusion.

5. a. Examine your writing after each half hour's writing and

note where you have failed to write the positive sign. Make the necessary corrections.

b. Remember that the negative sign which symbolizes the negative thought or habit you are trying to overcome will not be easy to eliminate or break. There will be a pull to return to the old way of writing, for it is easy to slide into old patterns.

c. You may find that you do not feel at home with the new way of writing and you may have a feeling of strangeness. Do not get discouraged and give up. Accept this feeling as a sign of progress. Personality changes do not come overnight; they require patient effort.

d. Every development takes time, and if it takes several months, or even a year, what is this time compared to the many years you have spent thinking and acting in a negative way? Persist and persevere and you will get the results you want. Epictetus said, "You must know that it is not an easy thing for a principle to become a man's own unless each day he maintains it and hears it maintained as well as works it out in life."

6. a. When you first start your new way of writing, write slowly to get the feeling of it. You can even exaggerate the change you are trying to achieve.

b. As it becomes easier to acquire the new sign in your writing, you need not exaggerate the change but strive for naturalness.

c. Increase your speed a little at a time until you can write the positive sign easily.

d. Keep increasing your speed until you can write the positive sign automatically.

e. This can usually be accomplished in two to three weeks, if you write regularly.

f. Then start eliminating or omitting other negative signs in your writing in their order of importance to you. Follow the above directions, but be sure you have eliminated the previous negative sign before you start on a new one.

7. a. In your daily writing, it is important that you use the writing exercise quoted at the end of each chapter describing the particular trait you wish to overcome.

b. These writing exercises are slogans, or positive self-suggesting thoughts; no thoughts, whether positive or negative, can enter the subconscious mind without the aid of the principle of self-suggestion. Slogans, maxims, daily exercises of thought, fine resolutions are easy to laugh at but not to be despised.

c. The subconscious mind means the deep self, and locked up in it is tremendous power and wisdom which can be made available to you in practical life.

d. One of the faculties of the subconscious mind is its ability to believe implicitly whatever the conscious mind declares to be the truth.

e. The subconscious mind responds best when the conscious mind is not confused with several ideas and comes to a clear-cut definite decision. It will then get behind you with all its wisdom and force and back you to the limit. It will always be on the job working toward the realization of your goal.

f. You think in words, i.e., symbols. Each silent thought is equivalent to talking to yourself, which is self-suggesting. Sometimes when you are alone, you may speak the word aloud. But silent or aloud, your conversation with yourself is creative and makes you what you are.

g. You can talk yourself up or down into happiness or unhappiness, into failure or success, into heaven or hell. The way you talk to yourself has a dynamic power for self-influence. Your words can make or unmake your life. "Nobody," said Cicero, "can give you wiser advice than yourself."

h. Self-suggestion, therefore, is one of the major keys to

personality reconstruction and self-mastery and is one of the best ways to change immature thoughts and habits to mature and positive ones.

8. Through repetition of positive, self-suggesting thoughts and affirmations combined with repetitious writing in a positive way, which works on the same principle, you have acquired a powerful double-strength method of achieving your purpose.

9. You must have faith that you will experience desirable results. It is only through faith and a determined act, i.e., a decision, that you can overcome your imperfect outlook or view of life. Your subconscious mind recognizes and acts upon your thoughts, and they must be mixed with strong positive emotion and feeling. "Faith is a state of mind which may be induced or created by affirmation. Repetitious orders to your subconscious mind is the only known method of voluntarily developing the emotion of faith," says Napoleon Hill in *Think and Grow Rich*.

10. Though it is beneficial for you to have your handwriting analyzed by a professional graphologist to see yourself as you really are, if you are an intelligent person you can understand and apply the rules and principles of graphology and the method outlined in this book for restyling or readjusting your personality through handwriting.

Is Your Willpower Strong or Weak?

It is by cultivating the will that men of genius are made, for all those higher qualities which are attributed to the intelligence are in reality qualities of energy and constancy of will.
—Jules Payot, *The Education of the Will*

Your character as an individual depends on your willpower and you will be either weak or strong according to the strength of your will. Your success or failure in life depends upon how you use your willpower. Your will is the power which enables you to regulate your impulses and feelings, control the activities of your mind, and to choose a definite course of action.

The element of purpose or aim is the first essential when you deal with the will, because without that there cannot be any pure will. After the aim is developed comes the intention to attain it, and then the motivation. The idea of energy is associated with the willpower, for the will is defined as a force which the thinking induces. Your willpower depends primarily on your desire. The greater the purpose and intensity of your desire, the greater will be your power of the will. Desire means an earnest wish or longing to possess or enjoy some real or supposed good.

Desire induces you to act and is the starting point of all achievement. If you find that your will is not strong enough to make the necessary effort to do the things you should do and what you believe is best for you, you lack sufficient desire for them. You can easily arouse and successfully stimulate a desire, even to the degree of enthusiasm, by picturing or visualizing in your mind the advantages or benefits connected with the matter over which you desire to exert willpower. If you do this conscientiously and persistently, you will find your desire growing rapidly. Backed by a strong desire, your will should act naturally and constructively with little effort on your part, and thus become well trained. This is the secret of accomplishment.

While every human endeavor requires that some element of the will be applied, we must differentiate stubbornness from willpower. Willpower is a positive force and is indicated by determination, resolution, decision, adaptation and strength of character. Stubbornness is a negative force and implies rigidity, changelessness and weakness of personality. Stubbornness is the cause of many health problems in the mind and body.

If you are an average person, or even if you are above average, you may find it difficult to keep fighting your tendencies to give up a hard task. However, you have to realize that you must continually exert effort of the will or directed energy if you want success in any path of life. There is no other way and the alternative is self-defeat. Life was not meant to be effortless. It is surprising to note that the will, which is the most important instrument for the attainment of happiness, intellectual power and success, and is the function most directly related to the self, is called an unknown and neglected function in modern psychology, psychiatry and education. We have been educated, taught and trained to do nearly everything, but we have not had an education of the will.

There are people who say they have no will. They do in reality have some will, for it is a direct function of the self, but it may be largely latent. Such people have to learn to use their small "capital" of will where it becomes an asset. There is no limit to the usefulness of an increasingly potent will. While the will can be trained, developed, strengthened and built up, it is not the work of an instant. Nevertheless, you must be ready to train your will and have an understanding of rules such as those given here.

How a weak willpower is shown:

	Example	Description		Example	Description
			How to correct:		
1.	t t t t t t t t	The *t* bar is: a. light and weak b. dish-shaped c. preplaced d. wavy e. varied.	1.	t	The *t* bar in the form of a cross with medium heavy pressure.
2.	i	The i dot is light.	2.	i	The *i* dot with medium heavy pressure.
3.	*others*	Light pressure.	3.	*others*	Medium to heavy pressure.
4.	*belted*	Slant varied.	4.	*belted*	One-way slant.

	Example	Description		Example	Description
5.	*abound* / *more*	Round writing.	5.	*abound* / *more*	Sharp tops of letters with round bottoms, medium heavy pressure.
6.	*he was far from*	Descending base line.	6.	*he was far from*	Straight base line or slightly ascending.
7.	*analyze the*	Irregular writing.	7.	*analyze the*	Regular writing.
8.	*There he is*	Wavering and varying base line.	8.	*There he is*	Straight base line.
9.	*finality*	Extreme right slant.	9.	*finality* / *finality*	Moderate, right and vertical.

How stubbornness (obstinacy) is shown:

How to correct:

	Example	Description		Example	Description
1.	*d t*	The *d* and *t* stem open (spread wide apart), pointed at the top.	1.	*d t*	Stem of *d* and *t* without points, closed.
2.	*t* *t* *t* *t* *t* *t*	The *t* bar: a. heavy b. downward slant c. downward, club-shaped d. hooked e. star-shaped f. down-curved.	2.	*t*	The *t* bar crossed on both sides of the stem with medium heavy pressure.
3.	*l t*	End strokes downward.	3.	*e t*	End stroke ascending.
4.	*e a*	End stroke with hook.	4.	*a e*	No hook on end stroke.

5.	*map*	Heavy pressure.	5.	*map*	Medium pressure.
6.	*men of*	Angularity.	6.	*men of*	Round bottom connections, sharp tops.
7.		Capital *L* terminating at the left.	7.		Capital *L* terminating at the right.
8.	*strike down*	Lack of end strokes.	8.	*strike down*	End stroke ascending.
9.	*p*	Lower extensions in small letter *p* ending in a left-turned hook.	9.	*p*	Small letter *p* with normal lower loop.
10.		Final left-turned in small letter *s*.	10.		Final without a left turn.
11.	*away*	Heavy downstroke in lower zone.	11.	*away*	Medium pressure in downstroke of lower zone.
12.	*as he could*	End stroke very heavy, thick and emphatic.	12.	*as he could*	End stroke with medium pressure, ascending.
13.	*opals are*	letters *r, o, e, s* and other small letters reduced to vertical strokes, and upper loops entirely discarded.	13.	*opals are*	Small letters clearly made, vertical strokes with normal loops.

Writing exercises:

1. I will diligently apply a positive willpower to develop self-discipline, decision, concentration and understanding, main-

taining constructive thoughts and emotions, using my abilities to accomplish my goal.

2. The following writing exercise helps to develop your will-power, self-confidence and self-reliance, enabling you to resolve inner conflicts, overcome fears, strengthen your positive traits and reduce the negative ones:
    a. Take a small sheet of white unlined paper (scratch pad).
    b. Use a soft lead pencil which will not break when pressure is applied on the paper.
    c. Write this sentence:

Take time to think today.

albert

d. Cross all the *ts* evenly on both sides of the stem with medium heavy to heavy pressure, one quarter down on the stem.
e. Sign your name and underscore it with two heavy lines as illustrated.
f. Do this writing exercise thirty times on thirty different small sheets of paper before retiring for the night for thirty days.
g. Do not skip one night and then try to make up for it the next night. You won't get results.
h. In any other writing you may do during the day, cross your *ts* as explained above and you will soon be surprised to see definite results.

As the emotions have strong power over the will, all writing exercises should be done with strong positive feelings and faith; then they will strengthen the self-suggestion from your conscious to your subconscious mind.

3. Imagination is a great ally of the will, as it is an aid to the development of strong thought habits. It also enables you to recall past events and marshal them before your mind for review and examination, to look into the future, and to construct plans. The following exercise or technique has been found successful in developing the will and is recommended by Dr. Robert Assagioli. Read his book, *Psychosynthesis,* a manual of principles and techniques.

Part A

1. Picture to yourself as vividly as possible all the unfortunate consequences to yourself and others which have actually occurred, and those which might occur in the future, as a result of your inadequate will.

Examine them carefully one by one, formulating them clearly; then make a list of them in writing.

Allow the feelings which these recollections and forecasts arouse in you to affect you intensely: shame, dissatisfaction with yourself, shrinking from a repetition of such conduct, and the urgent desire to change this state of affairs.

2. Picture to yourself as vividly as possible all the advantages which the training of your will can bring to you, all the benefits and satisfactions which will come from it to yourself and to others.

Examine them carefully, one by one: formulate these ideas with clarity and write them down. Allow the feelings aroused by these thoughts to have full sway: the joy of the possibilities that open up before you, the intense desire to realize them, and the strong impulse to begin at once.

3. Picture yourself as vividly as possible as being possessed of a strong persistent will; see yourself walking with a firm and decided step, acting in various situations with decision, focused intention, concentration of effort, persistence and self-control, resisting any attempt at intimidation. See yourself successfully attaining the desired ends.

Part B

4. To cultivate and reinforce the feelings and determination arrived at in Part A of this exercise:

a. Read selected literature that is encouraging, optimistic and dynamic in character, that stimulates self-reliance and incites to action. Best suited for this purpose are biographies of outstanding personalities who have demonstrated the best qualities of a strong but constructive will, or other books which aim directly at awakening the desired inner energies.

b. To benefit from such reading, read slowly with undivided attention, marking the passages which impress you. Copy those that are most striking and which seem appropriate to your case.

c. It is well to reread those passages several times, absorbing their full meaning.

d. After having engaged in such reading for some time, you will begin to feel a growing desire and you will even be anxious to set about the work.

e. This is the right moment for deciding, with all the firmness you can muster, that you will devote all the time, energy and means which are necessary to the development of your will.

f. Do not talk about this matter with others, not even with the intention of inducing them to follow your example. Talking tends to disperse the energies needed and accumulated for action. Your purpose, if made known to others, easily provokes skeptical or cynical remarks which may inject doubt or discouragement. As previously stated, "Good resolutions are easily laughed at but not to be despised."

g. Work in silence. This cannot be stressed too much.

The above exercise with its two parts constitutes one technique, or rather a method, having the aim of mobilizing other drives to enhance the quota of energy of will already available.

The writing exercises for the development of the will are first in order of importance in changing your writing to change your personality. When a positive will is established, you can succeed in accomplishing anything you desire.

Do You Procrastinate?

In delay we waste our lights in vain like lamps by day.
—Shakespeare
There is nothing more to be esteemed than a manly firmness and decision of character. I like a person who knows his mind and sticks to it; who sees at once what in a given circumstance can be done and does it.—Hazlitt

Do you find that when you are faced with a boring, disagreeable, tedious or difficult task you will make excuses to put it off for another time? One of the energy- and time-wasting by-products of a weak willpower is the habit of putting things off, or delay in starting or finishing a task. Procrastination and indecision are twin brothers. Where one is found, the other is usually found also. They reflect uncertainty and inadequacy, weaken the character, and are the most common causes for failure.

A procrastinator never achieves. He will have the following negative traits: indecision, a weak to vacillating willpower, and a lack of control. He will be hesitant, cautious and self-conscious and will have periods when he is inactive. He will be inhibited in some area, live in the past, lack self-confidence, and he cannot be depended upon. Even though he has good intentions, he never finishes what he starts.

Procrastination can result from having too many irons in the fire, leaving too little energy for a new interest. It causes restlessness, frustration, unhappiness and regret. It slows down comprehension and is not only an immature attitude but a failure-producing one. Psychologists tell us that parental overindulgence in the early years produces a dependent, discontented and emotionally immature person who cannot carry out any persistent effort. A person of decision is a person of action who possesses determination, intelligence and perception. Until a man decides where to go and what to do, he goes nowhere and does nothing. Decision is often the difference between greatness and mediocrity.

If you are an achiever, you will reach your decisions quickly and accurately and you will change them, if at all, very slowly. You will probably also have a good level of intuition. The secret of achievement or getting things done is doing it *now*. The habit of putting things off, waiting for the right time to start something, has caused many people to go through life as failures. Don't wait. You will never find a time that is "just right." Start where you are and work with whatever you have. As you go along, you will find better tools.

On the positive side, procrastination can break impulsive action and encourage second thoughts.

How procrastination is shown: Example	Description	How to correct: Example	Description
1.	The *t* bars and *i* dots are preplaced.	1.	The *t* bar crossed at both sides of the stem. The *i* dot directly over the letter stem.
2. *alter the*	Slow speed.	2. *alter the*	Moderate to fast speed.
3. *one two*	Beginning strokes.	3. *one two*	Omit beginning strokes to words.

How indecision is shown:		How to correct:	
Example	*Description*	*Example*	*Description*
1.	a. The *t* bar preplaced b. weak c. concave.	1.	The *t* bar crossed at both sides of the stem.
2.	The *i* dot preplaced.	2.	The *i* dot placed directly over the stem.
3.	Weakening finals.	3.	Strong finals.
4. *alfred*	Varying slants.	4. *alfred*	One-way slant.
5. *city of Boston* *city of Boston*	Wavering and irregular base line.	5. *city of Boston*	Straight base line.
6. *vine*	Hesitant beginning strokes with ink blob.	6. *vine*	No beginning strokes.
7. *fright*	Uneven pressure.	7. *fright*	Even pressure.
8. *share*	Hesitant and jerky connections.	8. *share*	Clear, even and continued connections.
9. *if the man was there at the*	Illegible script with inferior form level.	9. *if the man was there at the*	Legible script with superior form level.
10. *on top of*	Leftward slant.	10. *on top of* *on top of*	Rightward or vertical slant.
11. *the way*	Very slow speed.	11. *the way*	Moderate to fast speed.
12. *1969.-*	Useless and exaggerated punctuation.	12. *1969*	Omit unnecessary punctuation.

Writing exercises:

1. I will finish the tasks I have started with confidence in myself

and my abilities, knowing that decision is the first step toward achieving my goal.

2. The habit of putting things off is one that most people would like to eliminate. To help you get started, write a letter to yourself stating all the things you always intended to do as though they had already been accomplished. Don't stop there. Start doing them *NOW*.

What Is Your Self-Image?

In actual life every great enterprise begins with and takes its forward step in faith.—Schlegel

Unfortunately, most people in the world today suffer from inadequate concepts of self in some degree. This is crippling to the individual because it limits what he can do. It prevents self-realization and can even be responsible for emotional illness.

How do we get this way? We get this way by the lives we lead. In infancy, we depend for our health and psychological development on the quality of those around us. The people close to the child, having themselves been crippled, know no better than to continue this process. Few of us have had the opportunity to live the good life. That is, to grow up with people who respect us as persons, with whom we can have cooperative relations and become involved. The parents of some of the successful astronauts were asked in a questionnaire how they brought up their children. All of them stated that they always told the child, "You can do it."

When you are able to perceive the spiritual truth that you are a distinct and unique personality, that you are the only one who can do what you are best suited for, that you can answer a need no one else can, and that your growth and potentialities are unlimited, you will be able to recognize your worth and rise to meet it. Since you cannot realize your potentialities, whether in art, science or business, without sufficient self-esteem, you must do all in your power to rid yourself of the feelings of inadequacy; that is, those limiting, belittling, blaming and negative thoughts and attitudes about yourself.

Get a new concept of yourself. First, think well of yourself. Think well of others, too. See yourself as a part of a movement in the process of becoming and hence improving. Recognize that mistakes are inevitable. Develop and hold human values, and place yourself in a creative role. These positive concepts will enable you to adjust to and cope with any emotional stresses and anxieties which are intrinsic to the realization of your potential. Take inventory of the abilities and qualities your handwriting reveals and concentrate upon them. Raise your sights and aim at a goal you can accomplish.

Remember, no matter how able you may be and what other qualifications you may have, unless you have faith in yourself, you cannot use your abilities to attain any goal.

How inferiority feelings is shown:			How to correct:		
	Example	*Description*		*Example*	*Description*
1.	*I and Tom*	Capital *I* undersized as compared with other capital letters.	1.	*I and Tom*	Raise height of capital *I* to be same height as other capitals in the writing.
2.	*J*	The capital *I* without an upper loop.	2.	*l*	Moderate-sized loop on capital *I*.

3.	*Dear John*	The capital letters have the same height as the small letters.	3.	*Dear John*	Raise height of capital letters to be two and one half times the height of the small letters.
4.	*t*	The *t* bar placed low on stem.	4.	*t*	The *t* bar one quarter down on stem.
5.	*t*	*t* bar preplaced; it does not cross the stem.	5.	*t*	The *t* bar crosses the stem on both sides with medium heavy pressure.
6.	*write*	The small letter *i* is smaller than the other small letters and turns leftward, if the writing is rightward or vertical.	6.	*write*	The small letter *i* the same size and height as the other small letters, slanting in the same direction as other letters.
7.	*way*	A horizontal lower loop.	7.	*way*	Lower loops in downward direction, medium-sized.
8.	*outside*	Small letters uneven in size and height.	8.	*outside*	Small letters even in size and height (approximate).
9.	*because*	Small-sized writing.	9.	*because*	Medium-sized writing.

Items one to eight are the most important signs and you should pay particular attention to acquiring the graphic signs in the "How to Correct" column.

Writing exercise:

My thoughts will be concentrated daily upon the task of thinking of the person I intend to become. I believe in myself and know I possess the abilities to accomplish my definite purposes in life with persistence and continuous action.

Do You Have an Inflated Ego?

The knowledge of thyself will preserve thee from vanity.
—Cervantes

An individual who possesses an inflated ego that is so puffed with pride that he becomes vain and conceited, harbors superiority feelings. Such a person is preoccupied with thoughts of himself. He has an exaggerated sense of self-importance which makes him contemptuous of others, and he will look down on them as inferior. Boasting and self-satisfaction express themselves in his speech and he fishes for compliments. This is evidence of a mediocre mind.

Highly intelligent and cultivated people have too much sense to be conceited. They can see their own limitations and the ability of others reflected in the mirror of their good judgment.

Egotism, vanity and conceit annoy others and should definitely be toned down. These attitudes serve as red lights to warn others to keep away. The egotist wonders why he is unpopular and does not realize that his conceit is fatal to success. Shakespeare said, "Vanity keeps persons in favor with themselves who are out of favor with others."

Egotism, vanity, conceit and excessive self-confidence mask feelings of insecurity and uncertainty: the egotism is not on solid ground, which means that feelings of superiority in reality spring from an inferiority complex.

How an inflated ego is shown:

How to correct:

	Example	Description		Example	Description
1.	*I am*	Inflated loops in the capital *I*.	1.	*I am*	Capital *I* two and one half times the height of the small letters with an uninflated loop.
2.	*Robert Finn*	Large, also large and flourished capitals.	2.	*Robert Finn*	Capitals simply made two and one half times the height of small letters.
3.	*belivers have*	The small letter *e* is taller and more pretentious than the other small letters.	3.	*belivers have*	The small letter *e* is the same size and height as other small letters.
4.	*how like*	Inflated upper loops.	4.	*how like*	Upper loops normal.
5.	*joy*	Inflated lower loops, some in triangular form.	5.	*joy*	Lower loops of normal shape and size.
6.	*M*	Beginning stroke of capitals looped, right to left.	6.	*M*	Omit this beginning stroke to capitals.
7.	*M*	Capital *M* with very high first stroke.	7.	*M*	All upper strokes of capital *M* of even height.
8.	*L*	Base loop of capital *L* enlarged.	8.	*L*	Capital *L* with normal base loop.

No.	Left	Description	No.	Right	Description
9.	*better than*	Left slant.	9.	*better than*	Rightward slant.
10.	*John*	Signature overscored.	10.	*John*	Omit overscore to signature.
11.	*Mary*	Signature with underscore.	11.	*Mary*	No underscore in signature.
12.	*Martin*	Signature with overscore and underscore.	12.	*Martin*	Omit overscore and underscore to signature.
13.	*come*	Hooked end strokes.	13.	*come*	Omit hooks to e strokes.
14.	*m*	Capital *M* with uneven downstrokes wide apart and heads depressed.	14.	*m*	Capital *M* with all three strokes of same height and width.
15.	*More*	Large heavy convolutions to end strokes.	15.	*More*	Omit convolution to end strokes.

Writing exercise:

I have reasonable self-respect, being neither superior nor inferior to anyone. My own individual abilities and potentialities can be realized just as others can realize theirs.

Are You a Clear Thinker?

We do not keep the outward form of order, where there is deep disorder in the mind.—Shakespeare

If you are a clear thinker, you will have an orderly and organized mind and you will be a mature person. Ideas will not be confused or unrealistic, nor will they conflict. You will be observant and decisive; reason logically, strive for understanding, have an objective point of view and be able to judge a situation. In your business and daily affairs you will be practical, and you will possess poise, reliability and foresight. Your sense of proportion will be good and you will avoid making mistakes.

Those who think most confusedly are generally those who observe the least accurately. Most people go through the world with their eyes half closed and observe little. Your measure of intelligence is determined by your capacity to be observant. Neurotics are emotionally disabled because they do not know how, or do not care, to think clearly.

Acquiring well-established mental habits of simplicity, definiteness, and honesty of purpose will make you a clear thinker and safeguard you from vague, confused and indecisive thinking. You can stop emotional confusion and come to conclusions and possible solutions when you put your mind in order by examining and uncovering your present habits of thought with a view to ridding yourself of accumulated negative thoughts, feelings, habits, beliefs and prejudices.

Since emotional disturbances originate in irrational, illogical or unrealistic ideas, be on constant guard against mental carelessness, misinformation, indifference, hasty generalizations, superficial considerations, prejudices, and scattering of thoughts. The subconscious mind works best to help you in your endeavors when the conscious mind thinks clearly and makes a decision. Catherine Ponder in her book *The Healing Secret of the Ages* says, "Affirming order releases it to work in the subconscious where it eliminates that which is negative and weak. . . . It accentuates the positive which has an uplifting and healing effect upon the mind and body."

How confused thinking is shown:		*How to correct:*	
Example	*Description*	*Example*	*Description*
1.	Tangled writing of words and lines.	1.	Clear spacing of words and lines.
2.	Irregular and inconsistent spacing between lines.	2.	Regular, proportionate and consistent spacing of lines (also words).
3.	Sizable, uneven spacing between words; inferior form level.	3.	Moderate-sized and even spacing between words.
4.	Illegible writing, inferior form level.	4.	Legible writing, superior form level.
5.	Wavering base line.	5.	Straight base line.
6.	Blurred words, letters or figures.	6.	Clear words, letters and figures.
7.	Uneven pressure.	7.	Even pressure.

8.	*wearing*	Varying size of letters.	8.	*wearing*	Fairly uniform size of letters.
9.	*is it this he that*	Frequent undotting of *i* and uncrossed *t*.	9.	*is it this tie that*	Dot the *is* and cross the *ts*.
10.	*clea*	Illegible or neglected last letter.	10.	*clear*	Clear, well-proportioned last letter.

Writing exercise:

I will make a definite decision to realize my purpose by training my mind to concentrate, observe, think clearly and objectively. I will strive for order and understanding with right relations to all situations and people.

Are You a Deep or Shallow Thinker?

Thinking not growth makes manhood. Accustom yourself, therefore, to thinking. Set yourself to understand whatever you see or read. To join thinking with reading is one of the first maxims and one of the easiest operations.—Isaac Taylor

The habit of skimming the surface of things makes shallow or superficial thinking. Unfortunately, such thinking is encouraged today because it is the easy way. Most people are too indifferent or lazy to acquire facts with which to think accurately. They prefer to act on opinions created by snap judgments and will accept ready-made judgments on political, scientific, commercial, ethical and religious problems. Because our youth today are assailed from every quarter by our advertising age or predigested thinking, they are unconscious pupils of immaturity.

To acquire the independent, deep and accurate thinking which is mental (brain) power, you must first develop the habit of observation, then cultivate your own thoughts and intelligently organize and discipline them. Learn to investigate a matter thoroughly and carefully, distinguishing the essential from the unessential, and judge things upon their own merits.

Most people suffer intensely and needlessly from emotional conflicts within their personalities which prevent them from thinking clearly and deeply. Some of these conflicts are so severe that they need the help of trained psychiatrists. In many cases the individual can help himself and also strengthen and clarify his thinking by reading and studying books that explain the nature of the subconscious and how he gets himself entangled by his emotions. All of us have a great percentage of unused potential intellectual or brain power. It is said that the most we utilize is no more than ten to twenty percent. We should therefore spend more time in developing the brain. Reading and studying books by recognized authors on psychology, philosophy, metaphysics, biography, history, etc., will stimulate your brain to think, kindle your imagination and inspire you. When they have been read, dwell on them and ponder over them, and try to sense the thought, and keep your attention concentrated.

Just as exercise develops muscles, so does brain power increase by persistent and steady exercise. Such reading serves as an education and helps to forward your mental evolution. This should not be neglected if you wish to become a deep and accurate thinker.

How shallow thinking is shown:			*How to correct:*	
Example	*Description*		*Example*	*Description*
1. t	Dish-shaped or concave *t* bar.	1. t		Cross the *t* with a straight stroke on both sides of the stem.

2.	*money*	The letters *m* and *n* short in height.	2.	*money*	Increase height of small letters *m* and *n*, and sharpen tops.
3.	*M*	The capital *M* with middle downstroke that does not reach the base line.	3.	*M*	The capital *M* with all three downward strokes reaching the base line.
4.	*men manage*	Inferior or shallow, flat garlands.	4.	*men manage*	Garlands firmly made.

Writing exercise:

1. Use the first quotation and substitute the word "yourself" for "myself."

2. Write any passages from selected reading material that impresses you and seems appropriate to your case.

3. "Thinking leads man to knowledge. He may see and hear and read and learn whatever he pleases and as much as he pleases; he will never know anything of it except that which he has thought over, that which by thinking he has made the property of his own mind. Is it then saying too much, if I say that man by thinking only becomes truly a man? Take away thought from man's life, and what remains?"—Pestalozzi.

How Is Your Power
of Concentration?

If I have made any improvement in the sciences, it is owing more to patient attention than to anything else.—Sir Isaac Newton

Concentration is the ability to direct and maintain full and exclusive attention on an object without wavering or swerving. It is an intense mental activity, not a state of passivity. "The secret of mental concentration lies in the control of attention and the control of attention lies in the exercise of the will"—Manley Hall. You have to concentrate on the job at hand or you will not do it effectively.

You can learn how to concentrate your mind and awaken its hidden powers. By doing so, you can enhance the memory, will-power and inner strength that will give you clarity of thinking and efficiency in action. You will be able to do many things in a short time. Concentration also affects every other trait you possess. If you are a comprehensive thinker, you will be above average. If you have a temper, it will show a greater force and volume.

Most of us think of many things at one time. This divides the mind into many parts, giving only a portion to each thing. Therefore, we do most things with only a small percentage of our capacities. Once we learn how to eliminate the unessential, we can give our undivided attention to whatever we do. When you practice concentration, choose the object before you begin. Then do not try to hold the object in position by your thoughts. It is not the object that is going to run away; it is the mind that wanders. Let the object be thought of as in a natural position. This narrows the field of attention down to it, so you can look at it with perfect calm and without any tension or sensation in the body and mind.

If you are a beginner in concentration, you may often be annoyed if other thoughts intrude on your concentration. Be satisfied if you do not lose sight of your object, and take no notice of the intruding thought. Keep your emotions calm and the intruding thoughts will disappear when you are not looking. Calmness is necessary for successful concentration and you will find that it is not at all the difficult thing that it is sometimes supposed to be. When your mind is trained in concentration, it becomes one-pointed. This means that nothing will ever turn you from the goal you have set for yourself, and this is the secret of achievement. Dr. Erich Fromm, a psychoanalyst, was once asked for a practical solution to the problem of living. He replied, "Concentration for a half hour every day, twice a day, if possible. You have to stop in order to be able to change direction. Stop the mental and physical rush and you will stop being a stranger to yourself."

When there is poor health, emotional disturbance, inner conflict and oversensitiveness, there will be a marked loss or lack of the power of concentration. Well-adjusted people can concentrate even in the presence of disturbing stimuli. However, interfering stimuli of great force can affect the most balanced individual.

How lack of concentration is shown:		How to correct:	
Example	Description	Example	Description
1. *meant for*	Large writing.	1. *meant for*	Small writing.
2. *if long*	Upper and lower loops long.	2. *if long*	Upper and lower loops short.
3. *minute*	The *i* dots dashed and running away from stem.	3. *minute*	The *i* dot placed directly over the stem.
4. *t̄*	The *t* bar postplaced.	4. *t*	The *t* bar carefully placed on both sides of stem.
5. *bodily*	Varied slant.	5. *bodily*	One-way slant.

6. *[handwriting: can we]* Tall, wide letters, right slant, without pressure.

6. *[handwriting: Can we]* Small letters, medium heavy pressure.

Writing exercise:

I will focus my whole attention steadily and diligently on the task before me to complete it without swerving or wavering, keeping my mind and emotions calm and my body well, knowing that I can achieve my goal.

How Is Your Memory?

The secret of a good memory is attention and attention to a subject depends on our interest in it. We rarely forget that which has made a deep impression on our minds.—Tyron Edwards

A good memory requires accurate observation and clear thoughts. It depends primarily upon the intelligence and the amount of concentration one is possessed of. Memory has two divisions, the power to recall and the ability to recognize. In the average person, ability to recognize a word or a face is about three times as great as the power to recall the word he wants on the instant or to fit the face with a name. If you will observe carefully, you will find that your memory is not bad in all respects, because you remember with little effort the things that interest you and forget those that do not.

Since all of us forget the things we do not like, you should decide which are worth remembering. If you find something worth remembering, you should suggest to yourself the following thought: "I will pay attention to those things that should be remembered and will observe them accurately and think steadily upon them." Memory may be helped through training and exercise. A daily practice of even five minutes of fixing your attention on an object and observing all of its details, picturing them in your mind, recalling the previous day's image and comparing your picture with the object will improve your memory rapidly. In addition to improving your memory, this daily practice will improve your powers of observation, imagination and concentration, and enable your mind to function more effectively and usefully. The combination of this practice with the writing exercise will supply your effort (will) with double strength in attaining a good memory.

Those who have possessed a good memory often lose it when the health is affected or there are emotional disturbances, because attentiveness under these conditions is too difficult. While a cultivated memory is an asset, it is far more important to strive for the development of the power of thought and judgment. Amassing a quantity of little facts tends to encumber the memory, and a superior mind uses them as far as possible as notes. It isn't the quantity of facts that counts but the quality. This is often forgotten in higher education.

Memory ability is revealed by:

Example	Description	Indication
She went into this probability	Some disconnections in the writing, with light pressure.	A natural memory.
He had placed it before them	Well-connected writing, quick tempo, clear spacing.	Memory for logical connections or associations.
This type shows what could be	Moderately connected script. Light pressure, downstrokes simplified.	Memory for facts and circumstances.
How are we on a	Heavy pressure.	Visual memory.

How a poor memory is shown:		*How to correct:*	
Example	Description	Example	Description
1. *aid and aim it into*	The *i* dots omitted, misplaced or dashed.	1. *aid and aim it into*	The *i* dot placed directly over the letter and round.
2. *l*	The *t* bar omitted.	2. *t*	The *t* bar crossed at both sides of stem.
3. *a o d g*	Oval letters, narrow.	3. *a o d g*	Oval letters, wide.
4. *having*	Irregular forms.	4. *having*	Regular forms.
5. *my large phrewlas*	Poor spacing, lines entangle.	5. *my large pin was*	Clear, even spacing of words and lines.
6. *will they fare so*	Lean writing forms.	6. *will they fare so*	Full writing forms.

Writing exercise:

I will pay attention to those things that should be remembered and will observe them accurately and think steadily upon them.

How Intuitive Are You?

Men of genius are simply men who have dared to listen to their intuition.—Dr. Alexis Carrel

Psychologists agree that all of us function on at least four planes: sensation, which flows from the live senses; emotion; thought, the product of the intellect; and intuition, which functions from the others as they function from each other. In none of us are all these functions equally developed.

The supreme purpose of thought is to prepare it for the development of intuition. When the intellect is fully developed, thought moves into higher fields of concepts, i.e., mathematics, philosophy, music and other fields. Then the light of intuition irradiates the thinker's mind. Intuition is defined as immediate, unreasoned "automatic awareness," applying to people, circumstances, conditions and things. In *Psychological Types,* Dr. Carl G. Jung calls it "an irrational function, but this term does not denote something contrary to reason but something outside of the province of reason." In Jung's sense it has to do with "seeing around corners," with knowing things without knowing how one knows, with hunches and guesses as to what is going to happen next.

Intuition is a psychological experience called the "sixth sense," being immediate vision and direct knowledge giving quick perception and insight. By means of intuition one comprehends the whole and one is able to observe more in a situation or a person than may be evident on the surface. Only intuition gives true psychological insight into oneself and others. It is the highest form of understanding, wisdom and enlightenment, and also one of the greatest gifts in living, being a form of cosmic knowing. It penetrates reality and helps to get the truth of a matter quickly. With the help of intuition you can accomplish quickly that which would take a great deal of time under the slow action of reason and deductive thinking, and you will be able to avoid all the bitter lessons of life that come through blundering ignorance.

Intuition usually comes in flashes, i.e., they are fleeting and very easily forgotten, though they are quite vivid at the time they enter the consciousness. To write these intuitive flashes down immediately and then check them later would be a practical method of knowing whether our intuition is correct. Most of the great inventions and discoveries of science are the fruits of intuition. When asked what had been the secret for the development of his famous theory of relativity, Albert Einstein replied, "The really valuable factor was intuition." However, many intellectuals are to a certain extent afraid when intuition intrudes into their thought processes; they treat it cautiously, consciously or unconsciously; in most cases they repress it. But these are the people who have the greatest need for intuition, because as long as this precious function is left unused, they are incomplete in their development.

Valuable as intuition may be, it can only give limited results unless it is associated or combined with other psychological functions, e.g., logic and reason, which enable the individual to put his visionary ideas into effect. In addition, intuition should not be relied upon where the mental capacity, clarity of thinking and judgment have not developed enough to distinguish between true and false intuition. When there is a combination of intuition and mental activity, such as logic, sometimes the logical side steps in and checks the intuition; at other times logic acts as an augmenting power of intuition. The main trouble with this thinking is that it sets up indecision at times and also brings out unnecessary tension and irritability, especially over trifles. The individual is often in conflict, torn between intuition and reason.

Nevertheless, as Dr. Roberto Assagioli points out, "Harmonious interplay between the function of intellect and intuition works successfully when the intellect has the necessary function of interpreting and translating in acceptable mental terms the results of intuition, checks its validity, coordinates it and includes it into accepted knowledge."

While in every person intuition lies dormant, it is developed in few. To develop your intuition, you must be independent of the opinions of others. As it comes alive in quietness, there must be the use of the will to maintain a tranquil state of the emotions. Intuition does not reason with you; it just points the way and leaves you free to take it or leave it. In business, the logical steady thinker guided by reason is best, especially one who is practical, able to keep on a subject and complete what he starts.

How lack of intuition is shown:		How to correct:	
Example	*Description*	*Example*	*Description*
1. *the family was large*	Connected writing, with no breaks between letters.	1. *the family was large while claims that were made let like styles*	a. Disconnected superior form level b. connected, light pressure with shading c. sticklike small letter *l*.

Writing exercise:

"I am intuitive understanding;
Within me is the wisdom of the ages.
The mind that knows how
Is showing me now;
The mind that knows where
Is leading me there;
The mind that knows when
Will tell me then."
—From *The Healing Secret of the Ages*
by Catherine Ponder.

How Imaginative Are You?

We are all imaginative in some form or another for images are the brood of desire.—George Eliot

Imagination is the forming of images from memory by combining the elements of one's experience. It is a creative faculty and not a quality, for man can create anything he imagines. Your imagination exerts a powerful influence on your thoughts and acts, and affects your body. It helps you construct plans; it is a source of creativeness and is of prime importance in producing new theories, discoveries and inventions. It can look into the future, and your aspirations take form in your imagination.

Your imagination can be fertile, creative, inventive, constructive, ideal and inspiring; but it also can be impractical, fantastical, bizarre, romantic and erotic. It can lift you up but it can also cast you down. Do not confuse daydreaming or building castles in the air with imagination. Vague hopes and indefinite goals are not convincing to the mind. The only kind of imagination that is desirable for you to possess is that which can be put to practical use. Imagination is called the eye of the soul. It is one of your greatest gifts. It has motor power, and by directing your imagination toward what you want, you can transform every phase of your life.

Imagination requires the use of your will. It can be trained when weak and it grows through exercise. The more you practice the development of the mind, the more powerful will your imagination become. Picturing or visualizing a thing is the greatest secret for achievement, provided it is continually sustained, but it must not be forced. Holding negative images in the mind can cause mental illness. The same power that enables you to imagine negatively by picturing pain, guilt, and failure can also imagine success and freedom from pain. Psychologists tell us that some mental patients can improve their conditions by just imagining they are normal. The aim in doing this is to find the real self.

Lack of imagination is a major cause of failure in leadership, because without imagination a leader is incapable of meeting emergencies and creating plans by which to guide his followers efficiently.

How lack of imagination is shown:		*How to correct:*	
Example	*Description*	*Example*	*Description*
1. *if she will*	No loops in upper zone, made with a short straight line.	1. *if she will*	Long upper loops (in the mental and philosophical sphere).
2. *paying for*	No loops in the lower zone, short.	2. *paying for*	Long, wide lower loops (in the physical, material and sexual sphere).
3. *it is fine*	*i* dots low over the stem.	3. *it is fine*	*i* dots high and rounded, also made like accents.
4. *the stem*	*t* bar low on stem.	4. *the stem*	*t* bar high or over stem with medium heavy pressure.
5. *along the way to a*	Lean handwriting (lean in all three zones), angularity.	5. *along the way to a*	Wide handwriting, garland connections.
6. *favorable*	Connected writing.	6. *favorable*	Disconnected writing.
7. *laughing*	Lack of upper zone; middle and lower zone emphasized.	7. *laughing*	Upper zone emphasized.
8. *R W*	Tall, lean capitals.	8. *R W*	Tall, wide capitals.

Writing exercise:

I will exercise and develop the faculty of imagination in a practical and constructive manner, picturing and visualizing only what is best for myself and others, directing it toward the realization of my purpose.

How Far Has Your Specialized Skill and Knowledge Taken You?

Let every one ascertain his special business or calling, and then stick to it if he would be successful.—Benjamin Franklin

We are living in an age of specialization. Those who have specialized training and knowledge in all occupations are most sought after by employers. While you may have acquired a great deal of general knowledge, it is of no use to you in earning a living. Knowledge only becomes power when it is organized into a definite plan of action and directed to a definite end or purpose. Men are not paid for what they know but for what they do with the knowledge they have. "The function of knowledge is not merely to help you solve specific problems but to help you gain increased self-confidence through the experience of solving problems correctly, a self-confidence that frees you from the necessity of resorting to immature methods of proving your own significance."—Harry A. Overstreet, from *The Mature Mind.*

Employees who have ambition and study at night to increase their knowledge and skill in their particular work usually have qualities of leadership and many of them have risen to the highest positions. Chief Justice Warren Burger studied law at night. The way to success is continuous pursuit of specialized knowledge. Those who have stopped studying become mediocre. In any job, if you are without previous thorough training, you should first learn the qualifications required for the occupation you have chosen. If you possess such qualifications or aptitudes, feel that you will be successful and possess the will to accomplish, learn as much as you possibly can about it by study and training so that you acquire a technique. Most men who hold well-paid jobs have "the know-how" and they have worked hard to get where they are.

There are no shortcuts. Highly paid employees maintain a positive and generous attitude toward their work by doing more than they have to and they are rewarded better than they expected.

It is interesting to note that employers are now using "positive attitude" posters with a low-pressure human approach in order to plant the seed of a positive, constructive attitude toward a man's job and the company he works for. One of these posters, printed by The Economics Press, Inc., of New Jersey, shows a humorous picture with the caption, "Progress is when everyone pushes in the same direction. Lend a hand. Do more than your share."

While no one is born without some inherent ability, many emotional, mental and physical disturbances can be traced to an occupation for which a person is unfitted. While contentment in work is a capital factor, to achieve success in any field it is necessary for you to possess certain definite mental, emotional and personality traits as well as the physical condition required for the particular job. "Know your aptitudes," says the modern Socrates. An analysis of your handwriting can help you choose your vocation. You will know what your aptitudes are, whether you are suited to management, salesmanship, bookkeeping, art, mechanics, detail, etc. This knowledge plus specialized training will help you to realize a productive life.

How lack of specialization is shown:		*How to correct:*	
Example	*Description*	*Example*	*Description*
1. *long trips*	Long upper and lower loops.	1. *long trips*	Upper and lower loops short.
2. *young*	Long slender lower loops.	2. *young*	Lower loop short.
3. *realized this*	Uneven or wavering base line.	3. *realized this*	Base line straight.
4. *main*	i dot postplaced.	4. *main*	i dot round, placed directly over stem.

5. *where shall*	Irregular writing.	5. *where shall*	Regular writing.
6. *chosen*	Small letters uneven in size and height.	6. *chosen*	Small letters relatively even in size and height.
7. *ability*	Varied slant.	7. *ability*	One-way slant.
8. *having*	Uneven pressure.	8. *having*	Even pressure, heavy or light.

Writing exercise:

I will develop my abilities by applying myself diligently and with concentration to study and training for special skill and knowledge in the field of work I have chosen.

Do You Have a Clearly Defined Purpose in Life?

The secret of success is constancy of purpose.—Disraeli

It is said that 98 percent of the world's people lack a well-defined purpose or goal in life. This is not only a cause of suffering but a major cause of failure. Drifting about without a goal or purpose results in confusion, unhappiness and loss of interest, and you are bound to fail in whatever you do. You have allowed yourself to become a victim of circumstances and you will be a slave to the will of others.

If you wish lasting success, you must have a desire to do something and then develop a plan or purpose. You must know where you are going and what you are going to do when you get there. You must sense that what you are doing is of value. "Fulfill something you are able to fulfill rather than run after what you will never achieve"—Dr. C. G. Jung. After you have chosen a purpose and you are certain that you have chosen well and wisely, concentrate your energies upon it. Guard against subtle and alien influences that divert you from it. Make that single purpose your definite aim. When you take a positive action of the will to persevere in your aim, and you think constructive thoughts with a generous attitude toward what you want to accomplish, you can do anything you desire and believe you can do.

Many versatile people who, in their desire to do varied work, scatter their abilities, dissipate their mental and physical energies and become bored. No impression has time enough to become permanent because they lack the discipline to concentrate their efforts toward one definite aim or goal to achieve it. This leads to dissatisfaction, frustration and mediocre attainments, and they run the risk of wasting their lives in spite of their abilities. They always remain "round pegs in square holes" and most of them are "jacks-of-all-trades and masters of none." "This apparent power for varied work means nothing more than a great weakness of the will"— from *The Education of the Will,* by Jules Payot.

The most important thing upon which our happiness and success depends, the education of the will, gets little attention. It is not taught anywhere directly, and one of the weak spots in our educational theory is that young people are not given much insight into purpose. Few books tell us how the education of the will is to be conducted, and we pay little attention to anything but the stocking up of our minds.

How a lack of purpose is shown:		*How to correct:*	
Example	*Description*	*Example*	*Description*
1. *away from the*	Wavering or uneven base line.	1. *away from the*	Straight base line.

2.

t

t

l

t

t

The following
t bars:
a. light
pressured:
very little
purpose
b. rounded
top of stem
(no interest
in new
goals)
c. light
pressured
above stem:
daydreamer,
unrealistic
about goals
d. wavy, no
purpose, goal
changes
e. low on
stem: goals
low.

2.

t

t

l

f

t

a. heavy
pressured; sets
own goals
b. pointed
stems; goal
seeker
c. long, heavy,
above stem;
long-range
goals
d. looped;
persistence
in goals
e. one quarter
down on stem,
tall; pride in
high goals.

3. *of all the*   Uneven size and height of small letters.

3. *of all the*   Even size and height of small letters.

4. *healthy*   Varied slant.

4. *healthy / healthy*   One-way slant.

Writing exercises:

1. "There is no road to success but through a clear, strong purpose. Nothing can take its place. A purpose underlies character, culture, position and attainment of every sort."—Munger.

2. "I will make and put into action a plan to reach a definite goal. I will practice faith in myself and my fellowmen and God. I will tap the hidden powers within and above me. I will love and help people. I will work with all the energies of mind and body. I will know that I can achieve real happiness and success."
—Henry J. Kaiser.

Are You Preoccupied with Detail?

He who has the "spirit of detail" will do better in life than many who figured beyond him in the university. . . . Such a one is minute and particular. He adjusts trifles and these trifles compose most of the business and happiness of life.—Daniel Webster

To be successful in science, engineering, research and similar fields, you must have the ability to concentrate, organize and master the detail connected with your work. A Chinese proverb says, "The man who removes a mountain begins by carrying away small stones." However, those who are more engrossed by the details of a situation than by important matters have an immature attitude.

As the mind matures and gets down to essentials, it does not concern itself with unnecessary detail or preliminaries. It learns how to discriminate between the important and the unimportant, the useful and the useless, which results in efficiency. "A life devoted to trifles not only takes away the inclination but the capacity for higher pursuits."—Hannah More.

How preoccupation with detail is shown:		*How to correct:*	
Example	*Description*	*Example*	*Description*
1. *with Clara*	Beginning strokes to words and capitals.	1. *with Clara*	Omit the beginning strokes in words and capitals.

Writing exercise:

I will not allow unnecessary detail or useless matters to trouble me but will give due attention to those matters that are necessary and deserved.

Are You a Perfectionist?

Whoever thinks a faultless piece to see, thinks what ne'er was, nor is, nor ever shall be.—Pope

Dr. Leon Salzman, a psychiatrist, says, "It is not wrong to strive for perfection but the danger rests on the absolute need to do so and the inability to compromise once we have discovered that the goal is impossible." When an individual demands of himself one hundred percent achievement and feels dissatisfied and depressed when only ninety-nine percent is accomplished, his anxiety helps to make him a failure and leads to neurosis.

There are perfectionist parents who in their persistent demands and expectations of a higher standard of performance than the child can achieve, cause inferiority feelings in the child which he carries throughout life. When the parents withhold full acceptance of the child's efforts or outwardly reject him for not meeting this impossible level, the child learns to belittle his efforts. He believes that no matter how he strives, he could do better. This is the origin of perfectionism, which prevents an individual from having full satisfaction with himself and from carrying out any of his plans.

If you are a perfectionist who demands one hundred percent achievement, very strong discipline (willpower) can get you to accept the truth that no human being is perfect and that you must be content with achieving less than perfection. To function effectively and productively, you must be satisfied with being able to do the best you can, provided you exert an effort to do just that. You must also make every effort to reduce and abandon your belittling attitudes toward yourself, so that you will not strive so much for unattainable perfection. Develop a practical and realistic goal that you can accomplish. Seek the better, but shun the superman urge.

Make an honest inventory and appraisal of your personal assets and abilities; determine which ones you are best in. Then concentrate on them. These are probably the ones that give you maximum satisfaction. An analysis of your handwriting will give you the best clues to your aptitudes.

How perfectionism is shown:		How to correct:	
Example	Description	Example	Description
1. *l*	The *t* bar placed above the stem, light in pressure.	1. *t t*	The *t* bar medium heavy pressure above stem or one quarter down on stem.
2. *within a small*	Large size of small letters, with stereotyped regularity.	2. *within a small*	Eliminate this style of writing. Small letters should be average in size and not stereotyped.

Writing exercise:

Make an inventory and appraisal of your abilities as suggested in the last paragraph and then write the following:

I will concentrate upon those activities I can do best, with confidence in myself to carry out my purpose. As I know no one can be perfect, I realize that "he that does his best, does well."

Are You Thrifty or Extravagant?

Frugality may be termed the daughter of prudence, the sister of temperance and the parent of liberty. He that is extravagant will quickly become poor and poverty will enforce dependence and invite corruption.—Johnson

If you are a thrifty person, you have common sense and the power of resisting selfish enjoyment. The more you practice thrift, the easier it becomes and the sooner it compensates you when you save. It is indispensable to a successful career. Prudence is the dominating characteristic of thrift. It implies economy, alertness and keenness in making the best use of your money. "Economy is not a natural instinct. It is the growth of experience and forethought and is the result of education and intelligence. It is only when you become wise and thoughtful that you become frugal"— Grenville Kleiner, from *Make Your Life Worth Living*. Economy strengthens character and one can be both economical and generous.

Saving is an essential part of a thrifty person's life and he will not waste anything. Saving not only develops the spirit of independence and self-reliance but gives the satisfaction of knowing that you are providing for comfort and security in future years. Every victory over extravagance will give you a distinct moral uplift and raise you in your own estimation. If you manage to save five percent of your income, saving is a virtue; but if you say so much that you and your family cannot enjoy day-to-day living, saving is a vice. It is said that a hundred men can make money for every one who can save it, and a thousand men can save money for each one who can save it and keep it.

True economy doesn't mean saving scraps of old material but an ability to accomplish a great deal with the least effort, time and resources. Thrift overdeveloped or "going to seed" becomes avarice. Extravagance is completely opposite to economy. An extravagant person is immoderate, lacks caution and is a spendthrift who cannot succeed because he never really tried. Most extravagant people are luxury loving; many are vain, superficial and artificial and often misjudge, miscalculate and misunderstand. Others like to gamble and take long chances. Gambling, greed, miserliness, compulsive buying and get-rich-quick schemes are signs of emotional immaturity which produces negative emotions and undermines the health. There are people who in seeking to escape from inner turmoil will indulge in an extravagance. You've heard of the woman who bought a very expensive hat she didn't need after a quarrel with her husband.

How extravagance is shown:		*How to correct:*	
Example	*Description*	*Example*	*Description*
1. *as he*	End strokes very long.	1. *as he*	End strokes average length.
2. *I will do as he says*	Large writing, often with not more than three words on the base line.	2. *I will do as he says to a*	Medium-sized writing properly spaced.
3. *a tall man came in the room quite suddenly*	Margin on left side becoming wider as it descends.	3. *a tall man came in the room quite suddenly*	Margin on left side even.
4. *m*	Capital *M* with broad spaces between downstrokes on the base line.	4. *m*	Capital *M* with average width between downstrokes on the base line.

Example	Description	Example	Description
5. *did he do as he is*	Letters and words widely spaced.	5. *did he do as he is supp:*	Letters and words normally spaced.
6. *size 39*	Large, full, skillfully written numbers with heavy pressure, larger than script.	6. *size 39*	Legible, clear, nimbly written numerals, same size as script.
7. *Many of us were on a high ledge*	Wide margins.	7. *Many of us were on a high ledge*	Average width of margins.
8. *flying to Albany*	Lower loop letters run into line below (entangled).	8. *flying to Albany*	Clear spacing between lines.

How extravagance and thrift in splurges (erratic spending) is shown:

How to correct:

Example	Description	Example	Description
1. *The child was too near the pool when I first saw*	Margin on left side both wide and narrow, weaving in and out.	1. *The child was too near the pool when I first saw*	Left margin even.

*How overextended spending in the
beginning, then "hauling in of
the horns" to make both ends meet
is shown:*

How to correct:

Example	Description	Example	Description
1. *as it is for him and*	Words wide apart at the beginning of the lines, then pulled together at the end, often bent around the right-hand margin.	1. *as it is for him and*	Words evenly spaced on the base line.

*How forced inclination toward thrift
is shown:*

How to correct:

Example	Description	Example	Description
1. *Ann was at that place on the day we*	Wide right margin, narrow left margin.	1. *Ann was at that place on the day we*	Balanced margin, same width on both sides.

*How excessive stinginess
is shown:*

How to correct:

Example	Description	Example	Description
1. *at the end*	Hooks at end of strokes.	1. *at the end*	Omit hooks on end strokes.
2. *all we can with a*	End strokes short or clipped.	2. *all we can with a*	End strokes extended and rising.
3. *ten men were at that place*	Crowded letters, words and lines.	3. *ten men were at that place*	Good spacing of letters, words and lines.
4. *As far as he could see the clouds rose in*	Narrow margins on both sides or no margins.	4. *as far as he could see the clouds*	Medium-wide margins on both sides.
5. *is it Marys*	Poor punctuation.	5. *is it Mary's*	Proper punctuation.

| 6. | *m* (broken) | Strokes broken in small letter *m*. | 6. | *m* | No breaks in small letter *m*. |
| 7. | *The real meaning was not recognized* | Left margin narrowing. | 7. | *The real meaning was not recognized* | Left margin even. |

Writing exercises:

1. "The habit of saving is itself an education; it fosters every virtue, teaches self-denial, cultivates the sense of order, trains to foresight and so broadens the mind"—T. T. Munger.
2. I will exercise true economy and combine it with liberality toward those in need, yet I will spend less than I earn with faithful habits of work, service, study, meditation and carefulness in conversation.

Are You Acquisitive or Possessive?

Of the rich man who was niggardly and mean, he said, "That man does not possess his estate but his estate possesses him."

—Diogenes

In our society today, our sense of values is superficial. We are conditioned to the acquisition of money and possessions as part of the value structure. Ownership of material possessions becomes associated with a feeling of self-esteem. A person has stature and is judged on the basis of how much he possesses and not by the richness of his spiritual life. Seneca said of riches, "We are so vain as to set the highest value upon that to which nature has assigned the lowest place." Because of our false sense of values and our continual chasing after money and possessions as a be-all and end-all of existence, our very civilization is threatened. History has proved that great empires fell because of such false values. Possessiveness is the root cause of all war, tyrannies and many other obscenities.

Acquisitiveness is an immature attitude and is often acquired in the early years of life because of an unstable home environment that caused deprivation of something—love, affection, prestige or other securities essential to the individual's psychological well-being. The deprivation left uncertainty which resulted in built-in antagonisms, and there is a seeking for balance in material possessions, honors, etc. Usually such a person is an easy mark for the shrewd glib salesman or finance company.

Material possessiveness, which is a form of bondage, complicates our lives. To be continually looking at quantities of possessions confuses the brain. An inordinate desire or greed for possessions and wealth is avarice. Possessiveness causes all kinds of health and human-relations problems and is often reflected in stomach and intestinal ailments. When such an illness occurs, the power of elimination lets you know or warns you to let go of or eliminate some negative attitude, experience, relationship or possession.

Psychologists say that the average person is most of all in love with himself and clings to loved ones to gratify his own needs. This inevitably leads to possessiveness. The desire to possess people, or one person, defeats your real ends, restricts progress and leads to jealousy. We need to respect the privacy and originality of every human soul and allow complete freedom of development; otherwise the inner spirit resents the outrage of repression, and love dies. Strongest of all ties is that which does not bind.

If you will relax the mind, let go and loosen your grip on possessiveness by breaking your attachment to things and persons, you will be shown the way to a healthful state and will become a whole adult. No matter how you hold on, nothing will come permanently until you let go. "Wealth, after all, is a relative thing since he that has little and wants less is richer than he that has much and wants more. True contentment depends not upon what we have. A tub was large enough for Diogenes but a world was too little for Alexander"—Colton.

How acquisitiveness is shown:		How to correct:	
Example	Description	Example	Description
1. *averybigtent*	Words crowded.	1. *a very big tent*	Words clearly separated.
2. *young*	Very long (inflated), wide lower loops.	2. *young*	Lower loops medium-sized.
3. *fly cto*	A hooklike beginning.	3. *fly to*	No beginning stroke.
4. *ten ate*	Terminals short.	4. *ten ate*	Terminals extended and rising.
5. *one day*	Heavy pressure.	5. *one day*	Light pressure.
6. *m*	Small letter *m* with humps like ovals or half ovals.	6. *m*	Normally shaped small letter *m*.
7. *M*	Capital *M* with curling initial and end strokes.	7. *M*	No initial or end strokes to capital *M*.
8. *The first thing to do is to take a big piece of thin lin*	No margin on either side.	8. *The first thing to do is to take a big piece of*	Margins on both sides.

Writing exercises:

1. I will change my superficial values for true and lasting ones, finding pleasure in the simplicity of life, in creative purposes and doing something constructive for myself and others.
2. I will relax and let go all tension, stress, strain and all inharmoniousness of mind and body.

Are You Generous or Selfish?

A man there was, they called him mad. The more he gave the more he had.—John Bunyan

The selfish man suffers more from his selfishness than he from whom that selfishness withholds some important benefit.—Emerson

If you have observed generous people, you will find them to be the happiest, for they live a richer and more satisfying life than others. They not only share money and material goods but they give of themselves without expectation of acclaim or recompense. In their giving, generous people become strong because they have to exercise their power to produce the wealth to give, and life rewards them with wealth and honor. They prove the saying, "It is better to give than to receive."

Selfish people are mostly unfeeling and thoughtless. They look after their own interests, giving nothing to others. When selfish people are forced to give, they become irritable and usually ask themselves, "What am I going to get out of it?" Selfishness wants something for nothing and does not admit it. It takes many forms and when you think you have killed it in one form, it comes out in another. A selfish person cannot stop thinking about himself. "It isn't that he loves himself too much," said Dr. Erich Fromm, "but too little. In fact, he hates himself." Therefore he must grasp and devour every crumb of comfort he can obtain. As he greatly desires security, the absence of it makes him irritable.

Most of us have not learned that all our troubles arise from thinking of ourselves as separate units and then revolving around our own mental axis thinking of our separate aims, joys and sorrows. Selfishness is one of the components of immaturity. It is also ignorance. It is not a thing by itself but a lack of wisdom.

The lack of insight which makes selfishness possible should be discovered and corrected.

In searching for the truth about yourself, you may recognize your selfishness and become dissatisfied and even ashamed when you realize how your selfishness has brought harm to yourself and others. In this, there is a spiritual awakening of the will to attainment. You will enter a new level of consciousness and will aspire to rise above your faults. Out of these experiences a change will occur in your attitude, from getting to giving. Previously you lived to acquire, and now you live to contribute and cooperate. A great expansion of mind and outlook can be experienced. "It is for each individual to decide whether he wants to become a vital force for good and to realize that until he is truly living for the world and not for himself, he will never achieve anything that is thrilling, joyful, wonderful and inspiring"—from *The Finding of the Third Eye*, by Vera Stanley Alder.

How selfishness is shown:		How to correct:	
Example	Description	Example	Description
1. *at the beach*	End strokes short.	1. *at the beach*	End strokes long, curved, ascending.
2. *a cane*	Beginning and ending strokes with a hook.	2. *a cane*	No hook on beginning and end strokes.
3. *M*	Beginning stroke on capital *M*.	3. *M*	No hook to capital *M*.
4. *made for*	Left slant.	4. *made for*	Rightward slant.
5. *if he can he will try to*	Narrow spacing between words.	5. *if he can he will try to*	Wide spacing between words.

6. *all the men.*	Angular writing.	6. *all the men*	Curved or rounded writing.
7. *Harry*	Overscore and underscore in signature.	7. *Harris*	Omit overscore and underscore in signature.
8. *Marie*	Large, heavy convolutions in finals.	8. *Marie*	Omit convolutions in finals.
9. *Ann*	Final stroke circling overhead and enclosing name.	9. *Ann*	Omit this final stroke in the name.
10. *Mr. Jo Vr / 3 Elr R / Avn, Ohis 9 11*	Envelope illegibly written.	10. *Mr. Jon Doe / 5 Elm St. / Avon, Ohio*	Envelope legibly written.

Writing exercise:

I will always maintain generous and helpful thoughts toward others, for I realize that the truest measure of a man by what he does is by what he gives.

How Reliable Are You?

Give us a man of integrity on whom we can thoroughly depend; who will stand firm when others fail; the friend, faithful and true, the advisor, honest and fearless, the adversary just and chivalrous; such a one is a fragment of the Rock of Ages.

—J. P. Stanley

If you are a mentally mature person, you will be a reliable

person. No matter how much ability or other qualifications you may have, if you do not have reliability, you are no asset as an employee nor to your associates in business.

An unreliable person is one on whom we cannot depend, one in whom we cannot place our confidence and trust under all conditions at all times. Unreliability is associated with unpredictability. An unreliable person may be consciously dishonest but this is not necessarily true. Many people are unreliable because of emotional disturbances and not always because of a conscious wish to deceive and defraud.

If you are a reliable person, you will have a sense of responsibility; you will be stable, possess a strong willpower, perseverance, orderliness, good judgment, consistency of purpose, and you will not be easily influenced. All these traits are worth striving for, as they qualify you for leadership. If you obtain them you will be successful and universally esteemed.

How unreliability is shown:		How to correct:	
Example	*Description*	*Example*	*Description*
1. *in order to make*	Wavering base line.	1. *in order to make*	Straight base line.
2. *make it faster*	Irregular base line.	2.	Same as above.
3. *four hits and*	Uneven size and height of small letters.	3. *four hits and*	Even size and height of small letters.
4. *clarify*	Change of slant.	4. *clarify*	One-way slant.
5. *out of a*	Uneven pressure.	5. *out of a*	Even pressure, heavy or light.
6. *t* *t* *t*	The following *t* bars: a. dish-shaped b. preplaced c. light.	6. *t*	The *t* bar crossed at both sides of the stem with medium-heavy pressure.

Writing exercises:

1. I will approach my life goal firmly and steadily and will carry my responsibilities freely with constancy of purpose and reliability.

2. Write on lined paper for ten days, keeping to the line. On the eleventh day, write on lined paper and turn the paper upside down. If you are maintaining a relatively straight line, discontinue writing on lined paper. If not, continue writing on lined paper for a few days and test your base line again. Continue writing on lined paper until you can write in a straight line.

Note: When the base line becomes straight, you will find that your small letters become even in size and height and your slant will go in one direction. If you have also acquired a strong *t* bar, you will have acquired all the qualities of reliability.

Do You Deceive Yourself?

Nothing is so easy as to deceive ourselves for that which we readily believe but such expectations are often inconsistent with the reality of things.—Demosthenes

Most of us are generally engaged in mildly deceiving ourselves. Psychology has proved that we hide from our conscious minds the very things that cause our discomforts. Self-deceit is the act of lying and hence cheating oneself. It is a self-defensive mechanism which works against integrity and hampers comprehension. It sees only the external and results from lack of knowledge or a failure to get all the facts. It leads to rationalization. Ironically, he who is most possessed of this trait is the least aware of it. "The coward reckons himself cautious and the miser thinks himelf frugal," said

Homer. Self-deceit enables the unattractive, the timid and the grasping to carry on.

In one way or another, the average man seeks to escape the nightmare of his negative self and adjusts as best he can to his limited powers, resisting the forces which seek to vanquish his ego. Years of self-deception affect the health and lessen the soul. The lack of analytical ability or self-examination results in self-deceit. It is bound to result if you do not change enough to meet new challenges, and it will leave you with inadequate psychological tools. If you are self-deceptive, you have strayed from reality. Therefore, take stock of yourself. Write down your evaluations and keep them for later comparison. Be honest in detecting your short-comings and see yourself as you really are. Then balance your faults and failures with your good points and successes.

Put all your abilities to use. Set up a definite and realistic goal you can accomplish; use your intelligence and apply your efforts to realize it. Recognize the defense mechanisms that protect your ego from any disagreeable knowledge of itself. Get rid of your complexes, if any, such as an inferiority complex. Above all, never pretend to be other than you are, for all pretense is a hindrance to truth. This must be a realistic appraisal and self-examination. Most important, do not condemn yourself. We must realize that our conditioning, environment, education and tradition—and in many cases our own and another's ignorance—have made us what we are today.

Be content with what you are and what you have, and don't expect perfection from yourself or from others. Learn to accept the things you cannot change and correct bad habits that can be changed. This philosophy will give you insight and help you to develop new habits of thinking and behavior.

How self-deception is shown:		*How to correct:*	
Example	*Description*	*Example*	*Description*
1. *a e y*	Oval or circle letters with an initial loop.	1. *a o g*	Oval or circle letters without loops.

Writing exercises:

1. I will observe myself as I really am, with awareness of my strengths and weaknesses. I have faith in my abilities and in myself and will apply my efforts toward a realistic goal I have set for myself.

2. I will make a written list of my faults, choose one of them, and consider the best way to overcome it. I will take one fault at a time and gradually cover the entire list. I will do it thoroughly and honestly.

Are You Essentially Honest?

Dishonesty has many facets. It can consist of dishonest actions, dishonest statements, dishonest attitudes and expressions, dishonest feelings, etc. We will not go into the psychological aspects of the "why"—the reasons why people act dishonestly—since our concern here is with how much dishonesty can be detected, plus a possible means of changing that pattern of behavior. My purpose in this chapter is to show that the characteristic of honesty or dishonesty in a particular individual can be determined with a great degree of probability from his writing, and that the pattern can be significantly changed by following certain exercises and other training practices.

In a long period of working with the handicapped, Sol Zitter of Miami Beach has made a profound study of dishonesty patterns. He pointed out that dishonesty is not the same as lying, though it is similar. We can be dishonest while telling the truth and we can lie while being scrupulously honest. We can be dishonest with ourselves, concealing our real thoughts, feelings, desires, coating them over with more acceptable ones—one reason why psychiatrists and psychologists are so busy. We can be dishonest with money, power, politics, sex, friends, relatives, etc.

In this chapter we shall be concerned with conscious dishonesty which knowingly desires, attempts or actually carries out acitivities which are (or seem to be) for purposes of self-interest and against the interest of others. Dishonesty here is the taking advantage of another's trust in order to further self-gain.

Such dishonesty, in a very great majority of people, is accompanied by a feeling of guilt, a feeling that a wrong has been or will be committed. As with any feeling of pain, we try to alleviate it by rationalizations—reasons that will make us feel right in what we have done or will do. When we take stamps from the office for our personal use, we say to ourselves, "Oh, the boss expects us to do that anyway." When we take supplies, tools, materials or completed items from the factory to use ourselves or to sell to others, we say, "The boss doesn't pay me enough for my labor, and it's only fair that I should get more any way I can." When we manipulate our income tax or insurance claim, we say, "Well, everyone else is doing it, and anyway, I'm not getting much more than I should and they can afford it, since I've been paying them all this time." Even when we rob or steal, we may say, "Society [that faceless being] hasn't given me the opportunities I should have had, or the money, or the good times, and what I take from the person [that faceless being] I rob or steal from is only part of what I should have had in the first place."

In my research on the detection of dishonesty through handwriting, I have come to the conclusion that the feeling of guilt resulting from thoughts or acts of dishonesty manifests itself by certain handwriting peculiarities, by certain "negative" signs that can be recognized and analyzed by the experienced graphologist. It must be understood that such samples of handwriting being offered for analysis must be non-covering in nature—in other words, the subject, when writing the sample, must not know that it will be used by the examining graphologist.

Dishonest actions and lying often display themselves psychologically by fear, worry, and guilt feelings. The handwriting will reveal emotional upsets and the nervous tension which often leads to illnesses such as ulcers and high blood pressure. Such results occur when there is a conflict with the conscience, resulting in internal conflicts. There may also be a constant fear or dread of exposure, loss of job, desertion by client or customers, especially if the individual must constantly be on the alert to avoid detection.

Graphology, which reflects the subconscious mind, tells us that the subconscious in all of us is always truthful; it never forgets and cannot lie. It is the conscious mind which distorts the truth and drives us into all sorts of difficulties in its effort to fix things up. The basic truth in the subconscious speaks when the conscious mind is off its guard, as in the act of writing. Therefore, dishonest traits are revealed through some peculiar negative sign in the handwriting as indicated below. Before dishonesty can be determined in handwriting, at least four of the following graphological signs must be evaluated. This is because many honest people will make use of one or two of these signs.

How dishonesty is shown:		*How to correct:*	
Example	*Description*	*Example*	*Description*
1. *Let us know when to*	Wavering (sinuous) base line.	1. *Let us know when to.*	Straight base line.
2. *a a a a a a*	Ovals with loops or strokes within ovals, or with one stroke.	2. *a o*	Clear ovals, no loops within.

#			#		
3.	*a o d g u*	Ovals open at base of letter.	3.	*a o d g u*	No opening at base of letter.
4.	*o o*	Any unnatural opening as above, or at the left side of letter, e.g., *o*.	4.	*o*	No opening of oval at the left side.
5.	*will he do*	A covering stroke; up and down strokes overlap.	5.	*will he do*	No covering strokes.
6.	*your 31*	Touching up or correction of letters or numerals where legibility is not increased.	6.	*your 51*	No touching up or corrections of letters or numerals.
7.	*factor*	Pressure uneven.	7.	*factor*	Pressure even.
8.	*going*	Slant variable.	8.	*going*	Maintaining one slant.
9.	*answer*	Small letters vary in size and height.	9.	*answer*	Small letters relatively even in size and height.
10.	*to go the way of*	Writing that has many corrections.	10.	*to go the way of*	No or very few corrections.
11.	*⌣*	Very wide letter *m* (bluffer).	11.	*m*	Small letter *m* with normal width.

12. *let the party* — Increasing tilt of rightward slant at end of words or lines.

12. *let the party* — No tilt in right slant at end of words or lines.

13. *young* — Increased thickening downstroke.

13. *young* — Downstroke with same pressure throughout.

14. *trite* — Open *t* cross (deceptive, evasive).

14. *trite* — No large opening in *t* cross.

15. *3 2 4 8* — Numerals voluntarily indistinct so they can be mistaken for other numbers.

15. *3 1 4 0* — All numerals clearly written.

16. *if you are the* — Words and lines entangled.

16. *if you are the* — No entanglement of words or lines.

17. *because* — Decreasing size of letters in a word.

17. *because because* — No decrease in size of letter in word or increase in size.

18. *t l* — The *t* bars weak or nonexistent (weak will).

18. *t* — The *t* bars crossed at both sides of stem with medium heavy pressure.

19. *very truly, Martha F.* — Marked difference between script and signature.

19. *very truly, Martha* — Script and signature the same.

20.	*depedent*	Omitted letters (one or more letters left out).	20.	*dependent*	No letters omitted.
21.	*eacl* (*each*)	One of several letters replaced by letters that do not belong there, e.g., *eacl* for *each*.	21.	*each*	No replacement of letters.
22.	*g d a g*	Letters torn apart.	22.	*g d a*	Letters continued.
23.	*come m*	Slips of the pen, frequent starting of one word.	23.	*come M*	Strokes of word continued, no slips of pen.
24.	*way of*	Misplaced periods inside letters.	24.	*way of*	No periods within letters.
25.	*you got*	Lower loops distorted.	25.	*you got*	Lower loops made normally.
26.	*He was a good*	Consistent illegibility.	26.	*He was a good*	Consistent legibility.
27.	*A MAN oF*	Printed script unless required by one's profession.	27.	*A man of*	Cursive writing.
28.	*he was*	Snakelike finals.	28.	*he was*	Omit these finals.
29.	*lad But hand*	Exaggerated, artificial or flourished writing.	29.	*lad But hand*	No exaggerated, artificial or flourished writing.
30.	*———*	Slurring of letters.	30.	*many*	No slurring of any kind.

31. *[handwritten: framed]* Threadlike connections (adapts at all costs while intelligence can deceive).

31. *[handwritten: framed]* Positive garland or angles.

32. *[handwritten: A long walk]* More left slant in capitals and finals.

32. *[handwritten: A long walk]* Same slant throughout the writing.

33. *[handwritten: for New York]* Strokes turning leftward when to turn rightward is normal.

33. *[handwritten: for New York]* Strokes turning rightward.

34. *[handwritten: can you]* Connecting strokes in wide shallow garlands, weak pressure.

34. *[handwritten: Can you]* Garlands positively made.

35. *[handwritten: A,S, n r, E l sees roar Ease]* Writing of a letter in two different ways, e.g., now German, now Latin.

35. *[handwritten: sees roar ease]* Letters written in same way, or system.

36. *[handwritten: Those]* Left-tending strokes prolonged in loops and capitals.

36. *[handwritten: Those]* Omit left-tending strokes in loops and capitals.

37. *[handwritten: D R There]* Enrollment or curling of initial and terminal strokes.

37. *[handwritten: D. R There.]* No enrollment or curling of initial and terminal stroke.

38.	*H orr*	Counter-strokes (arcade form).	38.	*How*	No counter strokes.
39.	*you*	Smeary writing, lower loops ink-filled.	39.	*you*	Clear writing pressure.
40.	*ν = λ*	Simplifications of letters so that they become ambiguous and indistinct.	40.	*ν λ*	Simplified but not ambiguous or indistinct letters.
41.	*at the*	Slow, hesitant writing (lack of spontaneity).	41.	*at the*	Medium-fast writing.
42.	*paint the*	Arcades combined with angularity.	42.	*paint the*	Eliminate such a combination.
43.	*rove rove*	Arcade connections (flattened and appearing like garlands).	43.	*rove*	Garland connections.
44.	*going*	Threadlike endings or dwindling tendency in words.	44.	*going*	Clear endings of words.
45.	*m m*	Shark-tooth strokes pointed on last stroke.	45.	*m*	Omit the shark-tooth stroke.

46.	*from your going*	Lower loops too large, inflated, and entangled with line below.	46. *from your going*	Normal-sized loops, no entanglement of lines.
47.	*Sperling*	Signature illegible.	47. *Sperling*	Signature clearly written.
48.	*from a long*	Extreme left slant.	48. *from a long*	Avoid extreme left slant.
49.	*Mary*	Large-sized writing with thread connections.	49. *Mary*	Medium-sized without thread connections.
50.	*Muriel*	Calligraphic script.	50. *Muriel*	Natural writing.

Writing exercise:

1. I make my word as good as my bond, looking for the truth in every subject or question, cultivating accuracy of statement. I fulfill all obligations, whatever the cost. I consider a promise before making it, but once it is made I live strictly up to it, realizing that responsibilities rest upon me. "I consecrate my time, thought and abilities to a great life ideal"—Grenville Kleiner.

Are You Talkative?

They think too little who talk too much.—Dryden

Talkativeness is a pernicious habit. It exposes a person to the danger of blundering exaggeration and offensiveness. He falls into many mistakes and misunderstandings which judicious silence would obviate. A talkative person is not a deep reasoner. He is usually immature and gullible, quick to speak his mind and pour out everything he knows; hence he cannot be trusted to keep a confidence. Though he may be honest, generous and outgoing, he may tend to gossip and garrulousness. He lacks reserve and poise. The remedy for talkativeness is to put a strict seal upon the lips and resolve to cultivate a listening and receptive attitude of mind.

A mature person with an open, frank and communicative nature is usually truthful, sincere, generous, conscientious and a good conversationalist. He is more reserved than the immature, talkative person and knows when to talk and when to be silent without tactless indiscretion.

A reticent person is reserved. "Reserve," said De Quincey, "is the truest expression of respect toward those who are its objects." Judicious reticence is hard to learn because it takes many lessons in life to realize that speaking too freely often recoils on our own heads.

How talkativeness is shown:			*How to correct:*		
	Example	*Description*		*Example*	*Description*
1.	*a o d g s*	a. Small letters *a, o, d, g* open at top; small letter *s* open at bottom	1.	*a o d g s*	Lightly close small letters *a, o, d, g;* close small letter *s* at bottom.
	goad	b. with right slant indicates gossip.		*goad*	
2.	*d t*	Small letters *d* and *t* with a loop.	2.	*d t d t*	No loops on *d* and *t,* or small, narrow loop.
3.	*t h p*	Initial stroke instead of loop.	3.	*b h p*	No initial stroke to letters.

4.	*f*	Reverse small letter *f*.	4.	*f*	A positive sign.
5.	*halt*	Large size, angular connection.	5.	*halt*	Medium size and round.
6.	*too many do a half*	Some ovals open, some closed (person is sincere, neither very talkative nor reticent).	6.		A positive sign.
7.	*among*	Garland connections.	7.		A positive sign.
8.	*he is not so tall that he is*	Small uneven spaces between words.	8.	*he is not so tall that he is*	Small even spaces between words.
9.	*ammonia*	Shallow garlands.	9.	*ammonia*	Garlands firmly and evenly made.

Writing exercise:

I will think and reflect carefully before I speak, always using discretion in what I say to avoid offending anyone. I will talk when I have something to say, knowing when to keep silent.

Are You Tactful?

A quick sound judgment, good common sense, kind feeling, instinctive perception of character—in these are the elements of what is called tact, which has so much to do with acceptability and success in life.—C. Simmons

Tact implies delicate and sensitive perception, action and feeling and sympathetic understanding, particularly with reference to that which is fit, graceful and considerate under certain circumstances. It is a discerning sense of what is right, proper or judicious without giving offense. As a trait, tact is largely a birthday gift.

Tact makes life pleasant and agreeable and nothing so greatly helps to improve and maintain good relations among people. It also helps you to handle every situation that arises in your life. Tact differs from diplomacy. Tact is inspired by feelings and sympathy for people. Diplomacy is concerned with issues and implies ulterior motives, secrecy and shrewdness in dealing with others.

Tactlessness is a tendency to blurt things out impulsively without stopping to consider how it may affect others. Though you may be honest, candid and conscientious, if you are tactless, you are probably gullible and naive. Children often show signs of tactlessness; they speak out unreservedly because they lack the experience and judgment to apply tact.

How tactlessness is shown:		How to correct:	
Example	Description	Example	Description
1. *character*	Increasing size of letters at the end of a word.	1. *character*	Decreasing size of letters at the end of a word.
2. *a o d g*	Open vowels, or ovals, a, o, d, g.	2. *a o d g* *a o d g*	Carefully closed or slightly closed oval letters, a, o, d, g.
3. *roar*	Abrupt terminals or finals.	3. *roar*	Finals ascending to the right.
4. *also*	Large writing.	4. *also*	Medium-sized writing.

5.	$\mathcal{L}^-$	Postplaced *t* bar.	5.	t	The *t* bar crossed at both sides of the stem.
6.	*he went to the house but he did not see anyone*	Narrow or no margins.	6.	*he went to the house but he did not*	Margins on both sides, medium width.
7.	*follow the*	Hasty writing.	7.	*follow the*	Moderately fast writing.

Writing exercise:

"Talent is something but tact is everything. Talent is serious, sober, grave and respectable; tact is all and more, too. It is not a seventh sense but it is the life of all the five. It is the open eye, the quick ear, the judging taste, the keen smell and the lively touch; it is the interpreter of all riddles, the surmounter of all difficulties, the remover of all obstacles."—W. P. Scargill.

How Mature Are You?

A mature person is a craftsman in the art of living.
—Geoffrey Laytham, *World* Magazine

One of the great social deficiencies that the average adult suffers from and does not realize is an immature attitude or emotional retardation. Psychologists tell us that we are living in an adolescent civilization which is largely oriented to the interests and desires of adolescence even though these may be pursued by sophisticated techniques. Dr. Abraham Maslow, a psychologist at Brandeis University, says, "No person matures who is younger than 35." However, very few of us and perhaps none of us fully mature.

There is some area in our personalities where we still react as children.

People of intelligence do not always achieve maturity. Unfortunately, our society and our educational system do not yet teach us how to become mature. It is left to chance. While some fortunate people have received help to approximate a better maturity than others, it is generally incomplete. In spite of this, many people are able to sift through the falseness within themselves and arrive at their own individuality. "They succeed by forcing themselves to forgive more easily, doubt less readily, steady themselves inside and demonstrate tact outside. They establish order in their lives and find time for friendships, time for hard work and time to be gay"—*Love, Fear, and Anger,* by June Caldwell.

Maturity, then, is a matter of acquiring positive attitudes and habits by allowing your emotional energy to flow into constructive forms of behavior. The more mature you are, the more complete are your effective attitudes. The secret of maturity isn't the smothering or repressing of social emotions. It is the development of self-acceptance.

Maturity is also a matter of self-discipline to control your emotions and desires and attain equanimity. Equanimity means the balance or inward order that gives you the moral strength to accept life for what it is and get the most out of it. When such inner harmony is realized, you can face the vicissitudes of daily life. Unless one is willing to face life with all its disappointments, frustrations, joys, sorrows and anguish, one cannot expect to develop into an emotionally mature individual.

While you are what you are because of past influences and conditions, these cannot prevent you from applying new and effective influences for self-improvement, learning a new pattern of living, now and in the future. This learning pattern or process (growing up), which is a painful and tedious one full of temporary reverses, requires a certain amount of experience and observation. It depends above all upon facing the existential reality of our lives and somehow coming to terms with it and with ourselves. Therefore, every person can profitably ask himself, "How mature am I?"

"In what way am I still immature and how can I overcome it?"
You are mature if you:

1. Have developed self-acceptance, i.e., have a good ego development.

2. See yourself as you really are, i.e., distinguish fact from fancy.

3. Have the capacity to change and a desire to improve yourself.

4. Have developed a good willpower to control and discipline yourself.

5. Have the ability to adjust to unpleasant situations, to meet issues and to tolerate failure.

6. Can give as well as take.

7. Have the ability to maintain courage and determination.

8. Can handle guilt, hate and tensions.

9. Communicate with others in a meaningful way.

10. Have the ability to adjust to the responsibilities of marriage.

11. Get along and cooperate with others.

12. Understand another's viewpoint.

13. Have a mature sense of values.

14. Realize that perfectionism is inhuman.

15. Make the most out of your environment.

16. Have acquired independence of thought and action, self-reliance and a sense of responsibility.

17. Are living in the present.

18. Make your own decisions.

19. Have acquired mental and emotional stability and freedom from inner conflicts, self-pity and self-blame.

20. Enjoy being a good citizen.

21. Have brought your powers to realization.

How immaturity is shown:		*How to correct:*	
Example	**Description**	**Example**	**Description**
1. *our aim is*	Copybook or conventional type of beginning stroke.	1. *our aim is*	Omit the copybook type of beginning stroke (simplify).
2. *ℓ*	The *t* cross in the middle of a large loop in the stem.	2. *t*	The *t* cross on both sides of the stem.
3. *many*	Rounded letter forms (*m, n, h*); medium to large writing.	3. *many*	Sharp tops on *m, n, h;* angular, small writing.
4. *ability*	Change of slant.	4. *ability* *ability*	Maintain one slant or vertical slant.
5. *be ahead*	Short, very fat upper loops.	5. *be ahead*	Normal-sized upper loops.
6. *y*	Lower loops horizontal.	6. *y*	Lower loops in downward direction.
7. *bearing*	Small letters of varying size.	7. *bearing*	Relatively even size of small letters.
8. *longer*	Large-sized writing, larger than medium.	8. *longer*	Medium to medium-small writing.
9. *allies*	Uneven pressure.	9. *allies*	Even pressure, heavy or light.

10.	*bring*	Slow speed.	10.	*bring*	Medium-fast speed.
11.	*even size*	Long final strokes.	11.	*even size*	Final strokes medium length.
12.	*Sam Good*	Flourishes.	12.	*Sam Good*	No flourishes; writing simply made.
13.	*Sympathy allowing allowing*	Writing unsymmetrical or unbalanced in the three zones.	13.	*allowing*	Fair symmetry, relatively well-balanced in the three zones.
14.	*n*	Second stroke of letter *n* considerably higher.	14.	*n*	First and second downstroke same height.
15.	*g g g*	Lower loop to the left.	15.	*g g*	Lower loop complete at base line.
16.	*Can she do this soon as he will not be at home on*	Spacing of lines and words unequal in distance from each other.	16.	*Can she do this soon as she will not be at home on*	Spacing of lines and words at equal distance from each other.
17.	*I saw Bea*	Small and ineffectual capital *I*, smaller than the other capitals.	17.	*I saw Bea*	Capital *I* same height and size as other capitals.
18.	*t*	*t* cross postplaced.	18.	*t*	The *t* bar crossed on both sides of stem.
19.	*get to a place far and be*	Rigid, stereotyped regularity, large middle zone.	19.	*get to a place far and be*	All three zones balanced, no rigidity of letters.

Writing exercise:

I live in the present, make my own decisions, adjust to conditions and want self-improvement. I will develop self-confidence and become a self-reliant and responsible individual with determination to realize my potentialities. I will acquire a positive outlook on life, cooperating with others meaningfully, and maintain mental and emotional stability.

Do You Have the Capacity to Love?

Love alone is capable of uniting living beings in such a way as to complete and fulfill them, for it alone takes them and joins them by what is deepest in themselves.—Pierre Teilhard de Chardin

The words of a popular song these days say that the world needs "love, sweet love." It is something that we have "too little of." Unfortunately this is true, because most people can only love in small amounts; and when they speak of love, they mean getting it and not giving it. Psychology tells us that love is the youngest of all the emotions. Since most people have not yet met it and do not know what it is, it has to be learned and is a skill rarely learned before the age of 35.

No love, even maternal love, is instinctive or innate. Neither is all love healthy. It can be superficial and shallow. The best measure of good love is the emotional nourishment it supplies. If you love a car or a house, as some people do, it cannot love you in return. "We are shaped and fashioned by what we love," said Goethe. Mature love doesn't restrict itself to one person or even one family or nation. Genuine love respects every form of life, and this is the essence of morality. Mature love contains sexual desire as one of its components. Before a person can love maturely, he must first love himself and have a sense of worth. Hate is an outgrowth of self-hatred. Hate, resentment, anger and suppressed emotions produce sickness and can even kill if not neutralized by love. Buddhist monks are taught that hate does not cease by hatred but only by love.

As children reflect the emotions of those nearest to them, a lack of love or harmony between the parents causes emotional, behavioral and physical disturbances in children. Many neurotic conditions are hangovers from such childhood experiences. "Parents who know how to love their children without seeking gratitude or limiting freedom find they raise happy youngsters, free of neurosis and able to make their own way in the world. The children are successful in their work and in their love of life and never forget the parents whose wise upbringing brought them success and happiness"—Dr. David Goodman, psychologist.

People who know how to express love are healthier, age more slowly and live longer than bitter people. Love is the greatest of all healers because it is an uplifting emotional, mental and spiritual expression of divine vitality. Thoughts of love cause a beneficial change to take place in the body. They produce a positive current which dissolves opposite thoughts of hate and other negative emotions. By concentrating upon words of love, practiced regularly, you can transform your health, and this positive current can permeate your world.

Review the section on "The Small Letter g," which reveals the expression of love and sex in handwriting. You will notice that there is only one positive way of writing this letter to express normal love and sex relations, while there are many negative graphic signs. This is an indication of how few of us really have the capacity to love.

Writing exercise:
I will fill my mind with kind, helpful and harmonious thoughts toward everyone. Love heals and transforms my life.

Are You Sensitive?

Excessive sensitiveness is only another name for morbid self-consciousness. The cure for it is to make more of our objects and less of ourselves.—Bovee

If you are a sensitive person you will be easily hurt or offended, and very impressionable. Criticism of any aspect of your personal affairs hurts your feelings; you will thrive on praise and will always be alert for the approval or disapproval of others. Pride is what makes the feelings sensitive, and hurt feelings spur temper. Sensitiveness has a strong element of selfishness, and selfishness presupposes a sense of values which flows from immature reasoning. "Touchiness when it becomes chronic is a morbid condition of the inward disposition. It is self-love inflamed to the acute point"—Drummond.

Sensitiveness has its source in a weak ego. It accentuates gloom, depression and a sense of rejection, and it requires an outlet. When your ego is deflated, sensitiveness hits you somewhere in your body unless you have a positive philosophy to accept it. Independence helps to shrug off hurts, real or imaginary. If you have diplomacy, you will sidestep hurt-creating situations or tactfully prevent them from arising.

Sensitiveness is one of the flags of self-doubt. It feels deprived of understanding, encouragement and appreciation. It is not far removed from tension, because, being selfish, it will often be frustrated and this means tension. With strong feelings, well-developed sensitiveness neither wholly forgives nor really forgets. Practically everyone is sensitive to some degree in some area, as most of us have a weak ego; but it is usually sufficiently controlled to function socially. It is very difficult for a highly sensitive person to stand outside of himself to see the forest for the trees or to view a matter objectively and impartially.

An oversensitive person is unreasonably or morbidly sensitive and will often strike back at someone because his feelings have been hurt. He usually finds it difficult to adjust socially or in business. Anything said is interpreted as a personal dig. Always questioning the motives of others and looking for reasons for feeling angry, people like this lose their composure and there is a tendency to become too easily and often humiliated and extremely difficult to reason with.

Oversensitiveness causes a loss of energy; emotional strength is dissipated, intelligence is interfered with and integrity crippled. The oversensitive person floats above reality like a balloon. It is a lovely ride but an expensive one. The price is very high in terms of lost friendship, lost opportunities and loss of creative satisfaction. One must puncture the balloon with a knife of reason and float back to earth. On the positive side, a degree of sensitiveness should add color to life by heightening awareness.

How sensitiveness is shown:			*How to correct:*		
	Example	*Description*		*Example*	*Description*
1.	*d t*	The *d* and *t* with a fat loop usually twice as high as the small letters.	1.	*d t* *d t*	Loops to letters *d* and *t* with no loop or a narrow one.
2.	*d t*	When over-sensitive, loops to *d* and *t* are exaggerated.	2.		Same as above.

3.	Star-shaped t.	3.	Omit this shape from t and d. It is sensitiveness that strikes back with sarcasm.
4.	Open stem of the small letter t.	4.	Close the stem of small letter t.
5.	Open stem of the small letter h.	5.	Close the stem of the small letter h.
6.	Small letter i smaller than other small letters, indicating concealed sensitiveness.	6.	Small letter i same height and size as other small letters.
7.	Light pressure.	7.	Medium-heavy pressure.
8.	Very forward or extreme rightward slant.	8.	Medium rightward slant.
9.	Small m amplified.	9.	Small m normal size.
10.	Capital M simply made like an enlarged small m.	10.	Capital M two and one half times height of small letters.
11.	Nick in the small letter l.	11.	No nick in the small letter l.
12.	Sticklike letter l.	12.	This l has a positive indication.

| 13. | *Shadows* | Discon-nected, superior form level. | 13. | This is a positive indication. |

Writing exercise:
I will control my sensitiveness to criticism, applying reason, objectivity and a positive philosophy to accept it.

Are You Easily Irritated?

An ill-humored man is, almost of course, a selfish man, unhappy in himself and disagreeable to others. His chief pleasure seems to be to be displeased, if not with himself, yet with all about him.
—Anonymous

The definition of irritability is: an easily provoked, exasperated, impatient response to change in the environment. As tensions increase within us and around us, it is difficult to maintain a calm attitude. Irritability is caused by frustration and anxiety and disturbs the emotional tone. It may be basic and constant, or superficial and temporary. It can become a habit, and once it develops it will take over and control a person's life. The level of irritability varies from one person to another. Frequent outbursts of temperament will in the course of years destroy endocrine endurance and develop chronic fatigue.

Irritability results from boredom, conformity, fear of speaking out against injuries, unworkable goals and unworkable morals, social and cultural codes, and from the wide gulf between children and parents. Intelligent people are often irritated by mental slowpokes, having too many irons in the fire, and confusion. Irritability means that someone or something hinders the gratification of some desire, emotional or intellectual. The person who is always irritable usually comes from a poorly adjusted family in which there was little closeness and very little example of unselfishness. Growing up in such an environment, an individual has practically no inclination for the preservation of the larger values of life.

An irritable person is hypersensitive, plagued by the past; he is impulsive, jealous, has a fear of complexities and is often annoyed because he feels that he is less of a man than he should be. He is quite likely to be quick to observe faults in others and his irritability acts as a safety valve against pressure. An irritable person's emotions are stirred in a negative way and he does not know how to handle the situation. He suffers from a certain social ignorance and he has not been able to see through the network of his own character complexities. He will often lose a good position and never know why he was replaced. Usually he will look for other causes, such as prejudice in management or an office conspiracy, when the real cause was his own unpleasantness and emotional immaturity.

Such a person needs self-examination and enlightenment. He should stop and analyze himself and adjust to a more reasonable understanding of his problem. He must recognize the need to mature his own feelings so that they will be available as a means of enriching his life rather than a pressure to destroy it. He should learn how to control and direct himself, just as he needs to learn that success in every path of life depends upon the ability to control oneself.

How irritability is shown:			*How to correct:*	
	Example	*Description*	*Example*	*Description*
1.	*l* *l*	*i* dots in accent or dash form in either direction, pointed.	1. *l*	The *i* dot round, over the letter.

2.	*t*	a. the *t* bar is too long and heavy	2.	*t*	The *t* bar medium length and pressure.
		b. above stem or high			
		c. club-shaped.			
3.	*main*	Angular writing.	3.	*main*	Round writing.
4.	*measure*	Small letters, uneven.	4.	*measure*	Small letters, relatively even.
5.	*fore*	a. heavy pressure	5.	*fore*	Medium heavy and even pressure.
		b. uneven pressure			
		c. periodic pressure.			
6.	*it had*	End strokes short and pointed.	6.	*it had*	End strokes extended and rising (no points).
7.	*going to see my*	Entanglement of lines.	7.	*going to see my*	Good spacing between lines.
8.	*marking the*	Hasty; unequal size of letters.	8.	*marking the*	Medium speed, relatively even size of letters.

Writing exercise:

I will examine and become aware of my problems and my reactions to pressures and tensions and will adjust myself in order to stabilize my emotions with self-control.

Are You Resentful?

Resentment is a union of sorrow with malignity; a combination of a passion which all endeavor to avoid with a passion which all concur to detest.—Johnson

Resentment is a negative and immature attitude which can be conscious or unconscious and takes many forms. It is the "chip-on-the-shoulder" attitude which is an emotional reaction to a real or fancied personal injury or injustice which happened in the past. Resentful people are on the defensive, trying to shield or protect themselves against being imposed upon. They feel taken advantage of by others and often even anticipate it.

Resentment undermines the will, leads to self-pity, anger, hostility and quarreling, which makes a person difficult to get along with and is a failure mechanism. More people lose their positions and opportunities in life because they do not get along or cooperate with others than for any other reason. Harboring deep resentments because of a feeling of being imposed upon can do more to ruin your health and happiness than any other single trait. It is easy to start resenting a little, and soon the feeling grows and multiplies.

While there is a need to discharge resentments in some form, most people express their resentments in a negative way. However, if you can express resentments in a positive way by using your hurts and dissatisfactions as motives for changing your way of life to a useful, helpful or creative one, you have found the best way to success and self-realization. Dr. Roberto Assagioli in his book *Psychosynthesis* says, "One of the techniques for giving release to the emotions in a therapeutic way is that of writing." If you have strong resentment against someone, justified or not, it is suggested by the therapist to "sit down and write a letter to that person, giving free expression to all your resentment, your indignations, stating your rights, holding nothing back. Then burn the letter." This technique is more helpful than it may appear, because it involves the interesting mechanism of symbolic satisfaction. The unconscious is satisfied by the symbolic act of retaliation in writing. This should always be remembered because it is a very useful way to relieve emotional tensions.

How resentment is shown:			*How to correct:*	
Example	*Description*		*Example*	*Description*
1. *it was useful*	Long, stiff, rigid beginning strokes placed below the base line.	1. *it was useful*	Beginning strokes omitted.
2. *m*	A sharp top on the third or last upper stroke of the small letter *m*.	2. *m*	The top of the third downstroke the same shape as the first two downstrokes.
3. *f*	Sharp lower loop.	3. *f*	Round lower loop.

Writing exercise:

I am in right relationships with all people and all situations and will put my thoughts and energies to work to achieve a useful and helpful way of life.

Do You Feel Frustrated?

A splendid freedom awaits us when we realize that we need not feel like moral lepers or emotional pariahs because we have some aggressive, hostile thoughts and feelings toward ourselves and others. When we acknowledge these feelings, we no longer have to pretend to be that which we are not.

—Rabbi Joshua Loth Liebman

Frustration results when our desires are thwarted, unfulfilled or blocked, or when an important need or goal cannot be realized. This nongratification of desires threatens the personality, particularly the self-esteem and feelings of security. Self-realization is a universal goal and when we are blocked or frustrated in achieving it, emotional steam is dammed up. When it seeks an outlet, the excessive and misdirected frustration becomes a destructive force which can be directed toward those who cause the frustration or back at oneself.

John Dollard, a psychologist, stated that "the existence of frustration always leads to some form of aggression." This holds true for all needs. The more central and essential the need whose gratification is thwarted, the more intense the resulting aggression and hostility are likely to be. One of man's most important basic needs, which may be frustrated and which then unleashes intense hostility and aggression, is the need for love and acceptance.

According to Dr. Karen Horney, because our culture fosters intense competition and egotism, parents tend to possess a neurotic personality. The chief feature of this neurotic personality lies in the inability to love; consequently the child is frustrated in his need to relate to love. These feelings curtail the child's opportunity for effective personality development, making him an insecure personality and undermining his ability to function creatively. Carried to extremes, this leads to mental disintegration.

A small amount of frustration adds zest to life and may actually spur growth and successful creativity. But severe and prolonged frustration is a destructive force. Frustration is the normal lot of every human being and it is practically impossible to live and not experience frustration, anxiety and unhappiness. All of us have to go through life and meet its demands and we have to learn how to adjust to all the complex problems that occur in our lives. When we become aware of the causes of frustration, past influences and old patterns of behavior no longer wield so much influence. We must grow up and adopt a new philosophy of living, realizing that frustration is a negative attitude and as such can be changed to a less self-defeating way of looking at life. We can then learn to tolerate a certain amount of frustration without becoming upset about it. Finally, we must learn to redirect our aggressions and hostilities along realistic channels, and the best channel is working toward a practical goal within our abilities.

How frustration is shown:			How to correct:		
	Example	Description		Example	Description
1.	*ɑ ɑ ɑ*	Double curved ovals.	1.	*a, o d*	Clear ovals, no loops within.
2.	*a o*	Tightly knotted *as* and *os*.	2.	*a o*	No knots in *as* or *os*.
3.	*y g g*	Small letters *y* and *g* unclosed.	3.	*y g g*	Small letter *y* and *g* completed in lower loops.
4.	*gay*	Leftward slings of lower loops.	4.	*gay*	Omit the leftward slings in lower loops.

5.	*for fun*	Reversed lower loop in lower letter *f*.	5.	*for fun*	Normal loop to letter *f*.
6.	*Eli*	Exaggerated capitals and loops.	6.	*Eli*	No exaggeration in capitals and loops.
7.	*are*	Hooks and catches and backward movements to end strokes.	7.	*are*	No hooks, catches or backward movements to end strokes.
8.	*of all the*	Very small writing and heavy pressure.	8.	*of all the*	Small to medium-sized writing and medium pressure
9.	*stormed*	Wide connections and narrow letters.	9.	*stormed*	Connections to letters and letters of same width.
10.	PLACING A ROUND TABLE	Printed writing with heavy pressure, small size.	10.	*Placing a round table*	Cursive writing, medium pressure, medium size.
11.	*a sum of money*	Leftward slant, combined with heavy pressure, small writing.	11.	*A sum of money*	Rightward slant, medium heavy pressure.
12.	*on the top*	Narrow, close writing, large size.	12.	*on the top*	Medium wide, medium size.
13.	*Flora*	Signature encircled with large loop.	13.	*Flora*	Signature without encircling loop.

14.   *treat it*   The *t* bars short, crossed low on stem.   14.   *treat it*   The *t* bar crossed one quarter down on stem.

15.   *flat*   Varied slant.   15.   *flat* *flat*   One-way slant.

Writing exercises:

1. I will become aware of the causes and results of my frustrations and will not be influenced by past occurrences and old patterns of behavior but will adopt a new and positive philosophy of living by directing my aggressions and hostility to a realistic and practical goal within my abilities.

2. Just as stated in the chapter on "Resentments" psychologists recommend as a therapeutic measure to vent your feelings by writing a letter to the person who has frustrated or angered you. Pull no punches and express your feelings freely. Then burn the letter. This not only releases emotional tension but helps you understand yourself.

3. The following letter was published in the *Miami Herald*, July 5, 1970, in the Ann Landers column:

Dear Ann:

Last week, I was so miserable, I thought my world had come to an end. After a terrific fight with my husband, I wrote you a letter and signed it "Love and Hate." My letter was full of self-pity. I crackled with hostility and anger. As I read it over, I began to understand myself better—my feelings, my temper, my immature approach to settling differences. Seeing my thoughts on paper for the first time gave me a chance to view my problem as a third party might see it. It opened my eyes in a way that they've never been opened before. I did not sign my name or give you an address so I won't be getting an answer. But I really don't need an answer. I have solved my own problems and you have helped me do it.

Thank you very much—Hate Gone, Love Remains

Do You Have Unwarranted Fears?

Of primary importance in dealing with fear is the need of getting out into the open the object of our dread and frankly facing it. Human life is full of secret fears thrust into the attic and dark corners of our personality.—Harry Emerson Fosdick

The most destructive of all our negative emotions is fear. It is man's greatest enemy. In its mild form fear is doubt; in its most frightful form, fear is terror. It indicates a thwarted development. Fear makes us escape from actual living, prevents us from thinking clearly and from concentrating. It causes nervousness, sensitivity, insecurity, ill health and neurosis. Fear is such an intense emotion that if it is bottled up it secretes poisons in our system. Because it is a health and happiness wrecker, we must do all in our power to eliminate fear before it destroys us.

We are born with two fears, the fear of falling and the fear of loud noises, but by the time we reach adulthood, we have accumulated a multitude of others. Some of these are necessary for survival, such as fear of fire, precipices, etc., but most of them are not. We are afraid and worry over many things—poverty, failure, losing our jobs, not being loved, ill health, old age, death, etc. Fear is at the bottom of all our problems and difficulties. It is bred directly by misunderstanding, for whatever we do not understand is what we are apt to fear the most.

All of us want to be secure, but if we look deeply into life and its meaning we realize that there is no such thing as permanent security, because everything in life comes to an end. Fear originates in the mind in response to the anxious past and the troubled present. It doesn't exist by itself but exists in relation to something. Fear is the result of a lack of faith and a belief in limitations. Confidence overcomes the depression of doubt.

One cause of our fears is our own mental attitudes, wishes and projections coming back to us. Resentments, anger, hostility, hate, envy, prejudices and inadequacy do not stay buried in the unconscious mind. When these thoughts become conscious, they are intolerable because the superego magnifies them. If you will examine and analyze your thoughts carefully, search deeply into yourself and face your fears, you will see that these fears are false and unfounded and some are based on sheer ignorance. Knowledge and understanding and insight into yourself will remove fears. Once you have recognized and admitted them you will be ready to convert them into positive thinking. The most important basis of our fears is ill health. A fearful person is usually one who is less than well. A person in good health does not harbor fears.

The brain directs all our impulses and is the seat of our emotions and conscious thinking. As the brain depends on the body for blood and oxygen it must be affected by our diet, for what we eat determines the sort of blood we have. When the body becomes toxic because of improper food and improper elimination, the mental state becomes dull. We cannot think clearly, and there is a loss of memory and attentiveness; we are unable to face our daily problems and we begin to fear. Just as surely as you can banish fatigue, so can you banish fears of all kinds by creating a normal body in all its parts. In such a body, there is no room for either fears or fatigue. Correct your way of living and you will overcome emotional stresses and negative thoughts.

Nevertheless, fear has a positive side, for it is said by scientists that human achievement was attained by those who were afraid of being insignificant. Milton said, "Hope cannot exist without fear."

How fear is shown:		How to correct:	
Example	*Description*	*Example*	*Description*
1. *Wilbur dug his way*	Breaks in the upstrokes of the upper and lower loops.	1. *Wilbur dug his way*	No breaks in the upstrokes of upper and lower loops.

2. *and is* *and is*	a. Light pressure b. uneven pressure.		2. *and is*	Pressure medium heavy.
3. *for Mary*	Left slant.		3. *for Mary* *for Mary*	Right or vertical slant.
4. *Make two*	Wavering line.		4. *Make two*	Straight base line.
5. *in.d.s.*	Illegible script.		5. *enclose*	Legible writing.
6. *(al)*	Signature with circle enclosing it.		6. *al*	Signature without any additions.
7. *t* *t t*	a. The *t* bars light b. pointed, and heavy at the beginning.		7. *t*	The *t* bar crossing the stem at both sides, medium heavy pressure.
8. *enclose*	Extreme variations of small letters.		8. *enclose*	Relatively even small letters.
9. *if he is at the place.*	Wide right margin.		9. *if he is at the place*	Right margin average width.
10. *get your long*	Lower zone neglected.		10. *get your long*	Lower zone in balance with upper and middle zones.

Writing exercise:

I will correct my way of living and will have faith in myself, contemplating those things that are desirable and forgetting the rest. Thereby I will overcome fear, which will enable me to achieve my purpose.

Do You Have Guilt Feelings?

From the body of one guilty deed, a thousand ghostly fears and haunting thoughts proceed.—Wadsworth

Guilt feelings are operations of the conscience (the superego). There are times when the pangs of conscience are necessary and useful warnings of contemplated wrongdoing which should be heeded by that "still small voice" within the self. The function of the conscience is to judge the self. When there has been any conscious wrongdoing, guilt feelings should follow. This is normal guilt which is constructive because it can cause us to adopt new patterns for a healthy conscience.

However, when the pangs of conscience go beyond the normal guilt feelings or are exaggerated, rigid or unrealistic, they become injurious to the self. Such guilt feelings are generally more disturbing than anxiety and more difficult to dissolve. These destructive guilt feelings cause a loss of self-esteem, and create defense mechanisms, such as inhibitions and repressions which paralyze the will, resentments, fears, inner tensions, anxieties, self-punishment and mental suffering. All these prevent self-realization.

Nothing hinders personality more than abnormal guilt. Many young people are old for this reason. They are young in years but old in experience because their consciences have been overworked. When we fail to be what we deeply want to be, we feel guilty. The conscience condemns us severely for not making the most of our creative potentialities. This leads to hatred of self for wasting our opportunities and is the cause of serious mental illness. Self-condemnation is always self-defeating and should never be indulged in. There is no question but that all of us have done something which is not for the best and for which we feel ashamed. From this viewpoint, all of us have been sinners. If we have sinned, it is because we have been ignorant of our true nature and because the experience is necessary to bring us to ourselves.

To free yourself from abnormal guilt feelings you must carry your feelings to the normal verbal level and have a look at them. Awareness that normal guilt is constructive and abnormal guilt is destructive will help you recognize the choice you have to make between them. When one's inner conception of guilt is altered and becomes more tolerant, the willpower begins to operate creatively.

How guilt feelings are shown:

	Example	*Description*		*Example*	*Description*
1.	*t*	The *t* bar is postplaced (on the right side), close to stem.	1.	*t*	The *t* bar is crossed on both sides of the stem.
2.	*I was;* *I was*	The capital *I* is detached, e.g., the slant is vertical or leftward while the rest of writing is rightward.	2.	*I was* *I was*	The slant of the capital *I* is the same as that of the writing.
3.	*t*	The *t* bar made from left to right with down slant at the end of the stroke (self-blame).	3.	*t*	The *t* bar crossed on both sides of the stem.

Writing exercise:

I will do what is right with a clear conscience and be what I want to be by making the most of my abilities to attain self-realization.

Are You Jealous?

We are often vain of even the most criminal of our passions but envy is so shameful a passion that we never dare to acknowledge it.—La Rochefoucauld

The definition of jealousy is envy, suspicion and the demand for exclusive affection or attention. Jealousy's other ingredients are selfishness, imagination, exaggerated ideas and consciousness of inferiority. Jealousy, envy, avarice and greed are states of mind which arise from the desire to possess those things that are just beyond our reach. Jealousy is a form of fear that is difficult and stubborn. It is widespread and when continued destroys health.

There are three kinds of jealousy: competitive jealousy when an individual is threatened with the loss of a loved one; projective jealousy when fantasy assumes that someone is trying to supplant us in the affectionate esteem of another; and the more malignant paranoid jealousy which is so abnormal that it may be directed even toward some person belonging to the same sex and may be regarded as a defense mechanism against inadequacy.

Jealousy is as inconvenient as it is unpleasant. The average man finds it almost impossible to master, since by the time he is physically mature, jealousy's insidious poison has made him incurably immature in his emotions. This trait is so misunderstood that a person considers it an honor when his or her partner is jealous, assuming that it proves love instead of unresolved fear. Within every organization there is a great deal of destructive jealousy activated when a colleague makes a bit of progress.

Most people are aware of jealousy but prefer to ignore it rather than recognize it in themselves. People would rather die than confess to jealousy. While jealousy is not a profound study, the need to face it honestly is profound. We need to realize that "Jealousy lives on doubt. It becomes madness or ceases entirely as we pass from doubt to certainty"—La Rochefoucauld.

Most of us struggle with jealousy and fail. We try again and again, and no matter how hopeless the task may seem, we secretly believe that we will triumph over the great god jealousy. Jealousy is usually combined with other negative traits, e.g., jealousy of one individual, plus extreme resentment, plus temper may result in tragedy. Jealousy plus extreme depression can cause a nervous breakdown. Professional jealousy is often combined with conceit and self-deception. The reason for this combination of traits may be that a person who is professionally jealous is unwilling to admit the value of anything he fears will detract from his own efforts. He is conceited because of his feelings of self-importance and he is self-deceived because he is not as important as he believes.

How jealousy is shown:

Example	Description	*How to correct:* Example	Description
1.	a. A small circle on the capital letters b. a circle on small letters *b, c, e* (jealousy is directed toward one individual).	1.	Omit all circles on capitals and small letters.
2.	A large circle on capitals indicating professional jealousy.	2.	Omit all circles on capitals.

3. *will not be*   a. Uneven and wavering pressure
b. heavy pressure.

will not be

3. *will not be*   a. Even, medium-heavy pressure
b. same as above.

4. *⊘*   The *t* stem final incurved for a cross.

4. *t*   The *t* cross on both sides of stem.

5. *Bart*   Large inflated capitals.

5. *Bart*   Simple capitals two and one half times the height of small letters.

6. *big top*   Loops longer above the base line than below.

6. *big top*   Upper and lower loops the same length.

7. *Thought*   High flying *t* bars.

7. *thought*   The *t* bar one quarter down on the stem.

8. *a time for*   Incurving hooks at the end or beginning of words.

8. *a time for*   Omit all hooks to words.

9. *Clara.*   Signature overscored.

9. *Clara*   No overscore to signature.

10. *ι⁀ ι*   The *i* dots like accents.

10. *ι*   The *i* dots round.

Writing exercise:

I will strive against harboring jealousy and envy and will not be influenced by negative thoughts. Instead, I will keep my whole mind and my emotions centered on that which is loving, peaceful, good and joyful.